COWBOYS AND
INDIANS AND
PEGASUS DREAMS

To Wayne,
A long time friend ~
Blessings always to you
& yours!
Catherine Ann Anderson Kimball
Cathi

COWBOYS AND INDIANS AND PEGASUS DREAMS

Catherine Ann Andress

ELM HILL

A Division of
HarperCollins Christian Publishing

www.elmhillbooks.com

Cowboys and Indians and Pegasus Dreams

Published in Nashville, Tennessee, by Elm Hill, an imprint of Thomas Nelson. Elm Hill and Thomas Nelson are registered trademarks of HarperCollins Christian Publishing, Inc.

Elm Hill titles may be purchased in bulk for educational, business, fund-raising, or sales promotional use. For information, please e-mail SpecialMarkets@ThomasNelson.com.

Library of Congress Cataloging-in-Publication Data

Library of Congress Control Number: 2020904805

ISBN 978-1-400331192 (PaperBack)
ISBN 978-1-400331208 (eBook)

ACKNOWLEDGMENT

I deeply thank my lifelong friends who kept me going and who always gave me fun times and encouragement while I was making my stumbling blocks into stepping stones. There are other friends and family but these are my special dear ones which includes my little Shih-tzu, Zazu. May God richly bless you all as you certainly all have blessed me more than you can ever know.

Special Girlfriends

Cathy Hamilton Derr
Betty Britain Keith
Belinda Britain Lorenz
Waynel Lanham Sexton
Karol Baggett Zoellar

Special Married Friends

Tricia and Rick Allen
Sandy and Mike Hanner
Jody and Mike Harrington
Gail and Bobby Stephens
Toni and, the late,
Ralph Wallingford

"Schnood"
by Catherine Ann Andress

Man groped and he grumbled,
Stood erect and then mumbled,
"This thing I've created is good!"
He added flame to the fire,
Stood back to admire,
"I think I'll call it "Schnood"!

He decided to sell it
For a shiny gold pellet
Then he could claim it all!
When his child grew to giant,
He became most defiant
As he watched his empire fall!

He sat down to ponder,
To let his mind wander,
To 'things' that blazed in the sky.
He finished his task
Before he found time to ask,
"Who, now really, am I?

(Oops! He left out God!
And he was left alone to die!)

INTRODUCTION

This is the story of a third generation Texas woman born in a small town in the center of the Texas Panhandle. Over protected and reared to be a wife and mother just as all the women in her family had been, her goal became just that, to be a wife and mother and to have a family of her own.

Fate intervened, however, at every crossroad when her difficult first marriage to a rancher ended and she faced life as a single parent. After remarrying a few years later she was soon tragically widowed and, at 31, had to bury Kim, the man she loved so dearly. He was a Pathologist whose own terrible twist of fate occurred at the beginning of his medical career when, as an intern at Parkland Hospital in Dallas, he assisted with the initial postmortem exam on our late President John F. Kennedy. From that moment he was forced to live with deadly secrets which severely altered his life forever.

This story focuses on the author's great struggle to believe in herself to face the world alone and the unbelievable frustration of having to again and again tolerate and rise above numerous legal entanglements, drastic financial losses and, on top of everything else, employment injustices. All this while rearing her daughter with no one by her side to believe in her. In midlife, she was brought to her knees after a series of tragic events when she even prayed to die... this time she was led to the Great Throne of God's Grace.

In writing this she was able to revisit and immortalize those she loved so dearly after loosing precious loved ones tragically...a life impossible but for the grace of God and but for scriptures such as: Proverbs 3: 5 & 6, KJV, "Trust in the Lord with all thy heart and lean not unto thine own understanding, in all thy ways acknowledge Him and He shall direct thy paths"; and Genesis 50:20, KJV, "But as for you, ye thought evil against me, but God meant it unto good"; and Proverbs 16:3, KJV, "Commit thy works unto the Lord, and thy thoughts shall be established".

AUTHOR'S NOTE

I have a story worth telling. I hope that it is not too tragic and that I can project the humor I've been gifted from my father. I went through hell learning to survive these obstacles and I hope that by sharing these hard learned lessons I can help my own girls, and others, make giant leaps over the obstacles they encounter on their own life's journey.

I've changed a few names for privacy's sake and I refer to this book as a 'factual fiction with historically accurate places' for my own protection but I have not exaggerated at all. My purpose in writing this is to preserve special memories, share these lessons, heal my heart and to give all the glory to my Lord and Savior, Jesus Christ. I shall try.

It is with deepest love that I dedicate this book to my daughter, Leasa, my granddaughter, Brittney, and to Kim, who is just a breath away...and I commit it to the greatest Author of all, Jesus Christ, and I thank Him for helping me explore the heavy silence in my life.

CHAPTER 1

THIS SILENCE MUST BE BROKEN

I was born into an unusually silent home to parents older than most of my friend's parents. To an outside observer we had a lavish home and a very special lifestyle and we were quite blessed. I am not boasting with the descriptions of these blessings that follow but to show that we lacked for nothing except the most important thing in our home...we lacked walking with Jesus in our daily lives. And, as John 15:5, KJV, says, "I am the vine but you are the branches. He who abides in Me, and I in him, bears much fruit, for without Me you can do nothing." We went to church and I owned two Bibles. One of the most beautiful Bibles remained opened in our living room but we rarely, if ever, picked it up. Perhaps that was part of the silence.

When I was born my father, Barney, was forty two and my mother, Evelyn, was thirty six. I was their third child but, having lost a baby boy at birth three years before my birth, my parents were left with me and my brother who was eleven years my senior. I vaguely recall when my brother lived at home because he married and left for college when I was seven. I remember being sad and being very homesick for him when he left and I was elated when he and his wife returned for holidays and summers and stayed in our basement living quarters during his eight years of dental school. But for the most part, I was still very much the little sister who was probably tolerated more than anything.

My earliest memories are of our family's dinner table on Grand Street. I must have been a babbler even then because my brother, or "Bubba", I called him, would bribe me into silence...a nickel for every five minutes I could keep quiet. I would last only about three long minutes before I would burst into tears exclaiming,

"Bubba doesn't love me!" How ironic those words were because as an adult, time and time again, I came to realize that I was not loved but tolerated at best. And so this became my quest in life...to love and to be loved and cherished in return...but at the very least to be considered! I reached half my goal because I do love deeply.

One driving force came from a record album my brother brought home from college and shared with me. Much like today's educational tapes, we listened to this 78 LP record by Dr. Murray Banks who was a psychiatrist, I think. He used an amusing story, now an old joke, to describe the pessimist and the optimist. The one about the boy awakening on Christmas morning to be shown a room full of horse manure as his gift. Being the eternal optimist he jumped into all that manure and began digging and exclaiming, "WHERE THERE'S THIS MUCH HORSE POOP THERE MUST BE A PONY!" This was my first life gift from my brother...a lesson in keeping on keeping on. So this book is about my pony I call Pegasus, on whose wings I was "symbolically" lifted up on a lifelong journey to discover and embrace my Lord and Savior, Jesus Christ. My sister-in-law's gift was playing "What a Friend We Have in Jesus" on the

3

piano and her faith during the difficult and hushed waters I still don't understand but found our family swimming in for many years which, in hindsight, seems like it was always that way.

Except for my sister-in-law and two of my three precious nephews and their families and my daughter and granddaughter all these beloved people of my immediate family are now gone. I literally became like the boy digging in the manure and I just kept on keeping on in spite of often insurmountable odds and in the face of many broken dreams, heartbreak and among people who almost always let me down. All these losses have been almost more than I could bear but were very instrumental in bringing me to the Lord and to writing this book.

For the longest time I truly expected a few close friends and family to suddenly spring out of hiding yelling, "Surprise!!! This has been just a terrible nightmare but it's all over now!" Slowly I lost sight of this dream and the worse things became the more I believed I had to be getting close to the end of these hardships and heartbreaks! How wrong I was about that!

I grew up in so much silence. Where did all this silence come from? I'm sure my naivety was born in the silence and in being practically an only child by the time I was seven.

My father was a wonderful, one of a kind, self-made man who came to Borger, Texas, during the oil boom around 1926. One of eight children, he left school to help support his family and later worked as an errand boy in Dugan's Drug Store on Grand and Main. He then went to a six month long pharmacy school in Fort Worth while Mother worked to support them. He had to maintain a B average and, because he made one C, he had to repeat the entire six month course. When he returned to Borger he bought that drug store, got a license to sell liquor there and renamed it, "Barney's Pharmacy", after himself. He became a respected leader, served as mayor, became a bank director, worked diligently with A.A. Meredith to help him establish Lake Meredith, and earned position and respect in our small community which grew to a population of 25,000 in it's heyday.

My father also helped pay for a higher education for several people and provided a home for and helped support his parents until he died. He went from having very little to becoming one of the most successful men in town and had arrived at this destination when I was born. When I was turning sixteen I asked for a V.W. Bug like a friend of mine drove. He surprised me instead with a white, 1963, Ford Thunderbird saying he wanted me to drive a heavier car for protection. I also like to think he wanted me driving a car with a name that indicated flight and wings. He was a very generous but conservative man with a dry sense of humor which is why I think I was able to find humor in my life, which helped me enormously to get through it. I believe laughter is one of the best medicines.

Daddy died unexpectedly at sixty four which, strangely enough, I dreamed about the night before! I'd awakened in tears but I told no one about this dream remembering Mother telling me something about a superstition of hers about not telling dreams before breakfast or they would come true and I didn't want that. I'd forgotten about the dream until I got the phone call from my brother and Mother with the sad news later that afternoon. Following his funeral service many people I didn't even know came up to me to tell me that Daddy had given them free medicine and free rent from his rent houses when they'd hit upon hard times which was something I never knew until then and never would have known had they not blessed me with these wonderful things about him. And I'm so grateful they did. He was an amazing but quite modest man who never bragged on himself. He also taught me not to brag as well.

Daddy's father had been retired from the railroad for as long as I can remember due to an accident. The towns folk called him "Squeedunk" but I never knew exactly why he got that name. When we visited them Squeedunk would be in his chair and this also silent man would say, "And how are you today? Are you absquint or pucilanemous?"...which never failed to send me into the giggles. He had other special words, too, some of which I'm sure he made up. My Grandmother, Kitty, looked like the grandmothers in nursery rhymes with her comfortable bosom, rosy cheeks and white hair and she was always in an apron cooking something good up in her kitchen which smelled wonderfully of cinnamon and bananas. She called me "Catchie" and she gave all fifteen of us grandchildren silver dollars on our birthdays and at Christmas. In those days we had big family reunions during the holidays. My cousin, Francille, said her given name was Keturah, from Genesis 25:1, KJV after Abraham's third wife. I'm glad she shared that with me as I didn't know about it.

I must have been a caretaker by nature because I would frequently find little naked baby birds that had fallen out of their nests at Grandmother's house. I would keep them, name all of them "Henry", try to feed and revive them and when they died (they always died) I would bury them in pill boxes from Barney's Pharmacy. I had a big curiosity and I often dug them up a time or two to see if I could find them again. I remember taking a mouse out of the mouse trap in our garage and trying to pour cough syrup down it's throat which was the only thing I could think of to help make him better. I had an overactive curiosity which often got me into trouble and I was always trying to "fix" everything...to make things better if I could but I usually didn't have much luck with that. These are some of the things I found to do in the great silence. I also had three imaginary friends: Mineral Oil, Mr. Mack and a little Indian boy named Cutchie Coo, names I found amid the silence.

My mother was also silent most of the time. She always referred to herself as an orphan because she and her twin brother, Earl, lost both parents at an early age. Later in life I realized she felt like an orphan all of her life. Their father, Forrest, had been killed while working on an oil rig when the twins were only two years old. The oil company gave his widow $2000 and paid to bury him. Their Mother, Carrie, was left to rear her twins as a widow. She was a school teacher in a one room country school near Sedan, Kansas, where she started the twins to school when they were four to keep them with her while she taught school. She died four years later after thyroid surgery at Mayo's Clinic when the twins were only eight. She needed to have the surgery months prior to this but she insisted on waiting until school was out but, sadly, she waited too long and didn't survive the surgery. The twins went to live with their maternal grandmother on her farm, a tired woman who had already reared twelve (yes twelve) children of her own and whose husband, the twin's grandfather, died the month after her daughter, the twin's mother, died. Mother said she and Earl were so afraid they'd be separated if their grandmother couldn't take both of them and I think that is one of the saddest things for children to have to bear. Mother told sad stories of their childhood and their fear of upsetting their extremely strict grandmother who probably had no patience left and who believed that "children should be seen and not heard"...the most probable source of the silence.

I attribute much of my creativity and "wandering paths" to this silence. I was rather left to my own designs and allowed to explore and to do whatever I wanted until I got into trouble then I was punished and punished much too severely in my opinion. The problem was that nothing was ever discussed or resolved after the punishment and often I didn't really understand what I should have done instead of what I did do. I just suffered Mother's quick and severe anger with a switch off a tree or a metal spatula's burn on my bare legs over and over and over and I thought she'd never stop! I was so glad when it was over that I would apologize and run back to my room for yet more silence! This was always the case. I don't recall praise or encouragement and I was to learn by example and although they provided good examples to follow I personally needed some, or perhaps much, direction and guidance. I do not question that I needed to be punished but it was much too severe and followed with more silence. I forgave Mother for this because she had no gentle instruction herself so how could she give it to me? But I never stopped trying with her which was the birth of the "mother" inside me, I suppose. I believed, and I still believe today, that if you love someone you should never give up on them. But I have nearly killed my own spirit trying to do exactly that! Perhaps I just didn't know when to give up...rather when to give it to God and leave it in His hands! But I never even knew that was possible until much, much later in my life. I also didn't yet know that we need Him in our daily lives and that, "we can do nothing without Jesus", John 15:5, KJV, which is literally true!

I believe communication is the key to most relationships. Sadly I was not allowed to express my own opinions especially if they differed from my parent's. That was considered to be "talking back" or arguing with them. I have had important misunderstandings with authority figures and family in life because when I was growing up I couldn't find my own tongue during controversy or differing opinions without suffering consequences. All I knew to do was to bear it as long as I could then to finally stand up for myself with perfectly rational reasons and thoughts that needed to be expressed with a thundering heartbeat knowing that unless I agreed and kept silent I would, again, suffer severe consequences. The battle of self-expression would again be lost. The "silver spoon" I was supposedly born with in my mouth was silence...silence and over-protection and that silver spoon became a great handicap to overcome. Escape or rescue became my hope and I think that this was the birth of a "Cinderella complex" in me. (This term comes from Collette Dowling's book, "The Cinderella Complex.") Which brings me to Beatrice and why I like a sparkling clean house.

Beatrice looked a lot like Whoppi Goldberg's character in the Stephen Spielburg movie, "The Color Purple"...really, she did. She came to us when I was about six years old. The night before she arrived I dreamed about a little navy blue purse trimmed in red piping. This was my first 'Pegasus Dream'. The very next morning that exact purse was sitting on a table in the kitchen! When I asked about it Mother said it belonged to her new maid, Beatrice. I loved Beatrice and I loved coming home from school to find our home smelling of pine scented cleaner and furniture polish. I followed Beatrice around with my dog and polished furniture with her for fun. To this day I start cleaning house to work off nervous energy when I am worried or stressed out over something because I get comfort from the familiar fresh smells and from the ultimate results and often it was the only thing in my control during a crisis.

My dog, Puppy, and I made Beatrice laugh a lot and I played pranks on her all in fun but I was always well received by her. Daddy called her 'Madame Queen' which did not bother her a bit. Daddy loved all people and was not the least bit racist at all rather he liked to tease and have fun in a lighthearted manner and she didn't mind it a bit, in fact, she always just laughed at the attention he gave her. It wasn't until a few years ago that I saw on the front page of my local newspaper, "Madam Queen Comes Home" that I discovered that Madam Queen was the name of an old fashioned iron steam engine...so that's where Daddy got her nick name! (A compliment referring to her display of high energy, I'm sure!) He also told her she was welcome to help herself to a toddy from his liquor cabinet but to please not water down the Old Charter. We loved her like a family member.

One day I went with my brother to take her home and I asked to see inside her house in the flats which was where the Black people lived in those days. That was the saddest little one room house I'd ever seen but it was very clean but so dark that I could even see daylight through the boards in the wall. She had a husband who came and went and who beat her up a lot. She told me he even tried to remove the gold from her teeth and left her on the side of the highway outside of town. She came walking back home with my dog who'd sensed her plight and found her, I guess, as she walked back home and stopped at our house for help. I felt so sorry for her. My first taste of genuine compassion.

When Mother would punish me she would demand that I smile immediately afterward. That used to make me crazy that I had to smile after being spanked! Beatrice would

13

laugh at me and say, "Mrs. Barney done spanked Caffie, now Caffie's gotsta smile! Smile, Caffie, come on and smile, now!" And she usually made me end up laughing, too! She worked for us for many years then moved to Austin one day and I never saw her again. In college I occasionally shopped at a grocery store in Austin where many Black people shopped to ask around about Beatrice hoping to find her but I never did. She was the only person I ever knew who dipped snuff. I would heckle her until she would pull her lip down to show me the snuff because it made me laugh. Strange sense of humor developing here... but at least one was developing amid such silence. God bless you, Beatrice, wherever you may be. You were a dear and fun person and friend and you helped break the silence with your laughter. I loved you dearly!

When I was three we moved to the house on Austin Street which had few children my age in the neighborhood. Mother bought toys for me but I had no one to play with so I had to play alone a lot. I remember lamenting the fact that we didn't have a sidewalk that ran in front of our home like we did on Grand Street, which seemed to somehow unite us children together. So until I started school my cousins, Francille and Linda, and my first non-relative friend, Suzanne, were the only playmates I had. I was happy that

Mother sent me to half day nursery school when I was four but I was always more of a home-body and much rather be at my own home. Fortunately I had a terrific best friend in Susanne. Her family lived a distance from us but she and I became like sisters because our parents were good friends who had traveled together before we were even born. She and I had birthday parties for my dog, made lemonade stands in the summer, sold used funny books door to door and dressed up really crazy putting stuff in our hair and make up on our faces and put bandages and slings all over our bodies and would visit the neighbors acting like everything was normal. She had a younger brother and an older sister and Suzanne really knew how to have fun. I learned a lot from her in that respect. Her father, a physician, died of a heart attack when we were in second grade which was the first experience with death for both of us. Her mother's second marriage a few years later was extremely hard on her and she shared a lot about that with me. Suzanne died in 1995 from cancer and I cannot believe this funny, sunny girl ended up having such a horribly sad life and that she died so young. I thank her for sharing her fun loving spirit of discovery with me and for sparking my desire to understand why people do what they do to one another which was, I think, my initiation into psychology. I wrote this poem in her memory when she died:

Suzanne

Suzanne, Suzanne, child of springtime May.
Corn colored hair and bluebonnet eyes,
Pretty and funny, Suzanne.

Suzanne, my first friend.
Like sisters when we were little girls.
I see us in Hawiian grass skirts on Francis Street,
And being pulled down the hill on a blanket by
my pet Boxer.

I see you in your long skirts and hats tending your
garden,
Carrying cares greater than many must have.

Laugh once again, Suzanne!
Play in an evergreen garden in an ever blue sky.
And know that I loved you, Suzanne.

CHAPTER 2

PEARL LAKES &
GOOD FRIENDS

When I was four my parents bought a cabin an hour North of the tiny mining town of Creede, Colorado. Every summer we would take a couple of two week trips to Pearl Lakes Trout Club. Daddy would spend days packing his boat and Mother packed homey things for our cabin as we prepared for the eleven hour drive to the mountains. It was a log cabin without electricity or a bathroom when we bought it but we soon added both. I loved Pearl Lakes and my brother and his wife often brought their college friends up there. I recall I had an instant crush on their friend who taught me how to believe my dog, Puppy, had human thoughts and who taught me to converse for her. I can still hear him saying, "Puppy says..." followed with some really cute thought. This gift has given me countless, precious moments with all of my pets that I loved like best friends. I was so crazy about him that I wanted him to be my boyfriend! He was in college and I was about eight years old...my first love crush and possibly why I've always liked older fellows.

I'm very grateful my parents allowed me to bring a friend to the cabin with us. I first invited my cousin, Francille, then later I invited several other friends one at a time like Suzanne, Maryanne, Judy & Julia. In high school I got to bring Suzanne and Tricia and G., another one of my high school bosom buddies, so all four of us got to be there at the same time and we had an incredibly fun time. We always coordinated our trips with our friends from New Mexico who owned a cabin across the lake from us and who had two sons my age, Craig and Wally. We climbed all the mountains and made frequent hikes to the Ice Cave which was hidden high above Lake # 8 in Castle Rock. Fortunately we avoided any injuries as this particular adventure could have been very dangerous as the snow never melted up there and the entrance to the cave was a thin, narrow crack in enormous rocks with a slick, ice covered bump at the entrance. To get to that entrance we had to lie on our backs and go under a huge boulder then walk down a narrow path covered with about 3 feet of snow. We never entered the cave itself although I came very close one time, praise the Lord for a last minute bit of wisdom He sent my way! This became a traditional annual mountain climb for us but no parents ever went up there. Amazingly they just let us do whatever we wanted.

Craig and Wally had access to their neighbor's Jeep and we took that Jeep up mountains and logging roads where hardly any roads existed. One time we ventured into Creede and bought 3.0 beer when Wally, who was the oldest, was 18 and could legally buy it in Colorado. Even the half strength beer did it's damage in the high altitude. We wouldn't have been caught dead drinking beer back home because, like we were taught, nice girls didn't drink...not to mention the fact that my Daddy would all but KILL me if I did! But with a little encouragement from Suzanne, who was more experienced, and from Craig, who attended a military school and who was much more worldly than me and my friends, we broke our "Cardinal Rule" to never drink and we joined in a couple of times. (Craig reminded me of Mr. Magoo's nephew, Waldo, in the Disney cartoons. He even had those round, fleshy cheeks, which I called his "waldoes".) This is how I met Craig...who would become my husband someday.

Craig's Mother, Cloe, fascinated me. She was an artist and one of the most unusual and funny people I ever knew. She told wonderful stories and I helped her edit a book she wrote. Her gift to me was writing and making clay sculptures. She got a BA in Art from SMU and was quite good at watercolor but excelled in bronze sculpture. After Craig and I married Cloe made a figurine of me using the lost wax method and I often drove her to Prescott, Arizona to take her wax molds to a foundry where they made them into bronze. One of her acquaintances was Peter Hurd, the renowned artist, who lived on a ranch near San Patricio, New Mexico. She told me he once visited her home and critiqued her paintings and she made a life size bust of him which was in the Roswell museum for many years. She was my mentor in many ways and her art and her religion helped her keep her sanity...just as they would do for me in later years.

How such a sensitive, sweet woman as Cloe could marry such a verbally unkind man as Byce could be was beyond me. On one of our trips to Arizona she told me the bitter-sweet story of how she came to marry him. While attending SMU she met and fell in love with a man from back East. When they graduated he proposed marriage to her and promised that he would go back home and build a home for her and then he would send for her as soon as possible. He promised to write her often. She returned to her parent's ranch in Southern New Mexico to discover that her father had hired a ranch hand whom he wanted Cloe to marry. The man was Byce. This former car salesman quickly learned the cattle business and became one of the best cowboys on the ranch. I was told that Cloe's Mother and Father, believing that she needed a seasoned cowboy as a husband since they were going to give her a ranch someday, hand picked Byce to be that husband. This was in the days before telephones were commonplace and Cloe's Mother, she later learned, was hiding the letters from her fellow back East and Cloe thought he'd disappeared forever and she finally let them talk her into marrying Byce. The

21

Diamond Valley Ranch in New Mexico was a wedding present from her parents. I believe Byce had quite the silver tongue and she thought he was a kind hearted man when he was, perhaps, more cunning than anything else and I think this cunning later turned into bitterness from envy which brings me to Bootsie, the most probable source of that envy.

Bootsie owned a neighboring ranch to Byce and to Byce's brother's ranch. She was a character if ever I have known one. She grew up on a ranch in Texas and from the stories she told us I knew she had been a very hard worker and cowgirl as a young girl growing up. She told me how they cooked large meals for groups of cattle herders who came through with their herd always unannounced and often after they'd put in a hard day's work on the ranch themselves. She worked as hard as any man from childhood and they were very poor. One day oil was discovered on their land...lots and lots of oil which changed her life forever.

Bootsie was hardly five feet tall...a very small woman but she had the might and moxie of any man. She could be tough as nails when she needed to be but she had a heart of pure gold. She often left Cloe's bridge table to run outside and teach Craig to rope and if ever

Craig loved a woman it was Bootsie. She never had any children and I think she loved Craig as if he were her own son.

Bootsie and her husband built a fabulous Santa Fe style hacienda on her ranch. Bootsie always drove navy blue Lincoln Continentals with her name engraved on silver plaques on the front door of the cars. She smoked a small pipe with diamonds inset on the bowl. Each piece of her silver flatware had a sizable chunk of turquoise on the handle. When she received a shipment of bulls she would send one to Byce's brother. The same was true of feed for her cattle. She was extremely generous...more so than anyone I've ever known. I was told she was the first woman to be named Cowgirl of the Year in 1947, I think it was. She later became a judge for major annual rodeos. She once showed me her rodeo wardrobe. Gene Autry's tailor designed and made her rodeo suits... western suits so heavily studded with sequins and faux jewels that they weighed over twenty pounds and she owned dozens of them. I was blessed to get to watch Cloe make a bronze statue of Bootsie in her Western attire holding her dainty pipe in her hand which she submitted for acceptance to the Cowboy Hall of Fame in Oklahoma City before women and cowgirls had been accepted there. I wish I knew more about this.

Bootsie was a staunch Democrat much to Byce's chagrin. I also was told she hosted a benefit for Kennedy and Johnson at her ranch when they ran for office and that both Kennedy and Johnson flew in by helicopter for the event. (This was the second "near-brush" with JFK I was to have in my lifetime.) I believe that this ultra lavish lifestyle Bootsie was living evoked a bit of envy in Byce. Although Byce and Cloe were quite comfortable working cattle is a hard way to earn a living and Bootsie's lifestyle exceeded everyone else's by far. So Byce began sinking every spare dime he had into one dry hole after another and became more bitter with each loss. He was being beaten...and by a woman, no less!

Byce looked very much like Richard Boone in the old Paladin television series in the '60's and he could be as mean as an old rattlesnake! I knew Craig and Wally feared him because they told me themselves but I never realized how much they really feared him until I married into the family. He was irrational, loud and negative all the time! When Craig was around six years old he got stepped on by a bull nearly severing his toe but he was so afraid to tell Byce that he worked the rest of the day with a blood filled boot and never said a word to him about his injury fearing his father's rage! I believe a hardness was forming deep inside him. Cloe told me that when Wally was only two years old Byce left him standing on the edge of a high precipice just to see what he would do! Byce said, "if the boy has any sense at all he won't move an inch and if he falls he wasn't worth keeping anyway!" I could hardly fathom that he was really like that...but he was.

I was stunned into silence, myself, the first several times I observed Byce fussing at Cloe while she was cooking breakfast over whether to put eggs in the pancakes or not! It was constant ranting and raving and it was absolutely unbearable!!! Cloe eventually divorced him in later years and no one could blame her. Byce's verbal abuse was endless from daylight to dark and "all the live long day" (just like "The Eyes of Texas", my alma mater's song, says!) I once asked Cloe how she tolerated his constant verbal abuse and she said she'd learned to shut him out by praying the Hail Mary prayer over and over the whole time he raged on and on at her. I've read stories about children who are treated this way who strive to please their abusing parent out of hunger for praise from them. This seemed to be true in Craig's

25

case, in my opinion anyway. I honestly believe Byce only had one or two good days a year and this was when he was thrust among people so he wanted to act nicely. He had an amazing chameleon like ability to become most gracious in public and unless you saw it first hand you would never suspect his cruelty. Strangely enough, Bootsie and Byce died on the same day in 1993, I think it was. I was told she died while riding in a rodeo in San Antonio, Texas, and that Craig was there and saw it happen then he had the dutiful honor of bringing her back home for the last time. An extremely sad day for him, I'm sure.

Cloe's father owned the Running Horse Ranch in southern New Mexico. I only visited the Running Horse once after Craig and I were married. I was amazed when I saw this ranch! It had board sidewalks and three good sized homes where Cloe's parents lived and where her two brothers eventually made their own homes with their wives and children. It even had it's own post office! It very much resembled a town from western movie scenes and was actually on the map just like a town. Cloe told me that her father brought a special breed of long haired sheep from another country to the United States and formed a company that established telephone exchanges and airports in Texas. Quite an accomplished man. He and one of his sons were killed in his plane in a crash on the ranch when Craig was only two days old. This upset Cloe so much that she left Craig in the hospital where he was born to return to the ranch to be with her family. It was not as easy to travel in those days and Cloe, having the mind of an artist, was easily distracted and engrossed in things. However she left him there much too long...in fact when the hospital called her and asked her to please pick him up he was eight months old and the oldest baby in the nursery! This saddens me a lot. In those days nurses did not know how vitally important it is to bond with babies and I imagine he was only fed and changed and left alone a lot. I believe this greatly affected his personality and I doubt if Craig ever truly knew how to show love and tenderness. Thanks to one of his cousins who came to see us for the sole purpose of telling my daughter that he really was left in the hospital for 8 months after his birth which is very difficult to believe, I found out that there was a nurse who loved him and who begged to adopt him but Cloe refused to let her. Knowing this helped soothe the heartache and sympathy I had for baby Craig. Just knowing he was loved those eight long months gave me some comfort.

27

However the abrupt separation from this nurse forever had to be another heartbreaking loss for eight month old baby Craig.

Craig and I saw each other only during the summers at Pearl Lakes from the time we were six or seven years old and it wasn't until high school that we visited each other's homes. Mother and my girl friend, Judy's, mother and sister, drove us to a school dance at Craig's and Wally's military school in New Mexico one year. And Cloe and Mother took us all to New York the summer of 1964, for the World's Fair. We were silly, playful, full of laughter and always having fun...more fun than I think I had ever had with any boy but we were never romantically involved. We were always just very good friends.

It was in high school I finally found my way out of the silence. I had lost my chubbiness, outgrew my childhood asthma and the ugly duckling stages of adolescence and found myself to be a happy and outgoing person. It always surprised me when friends came easily and contests were won easily. I was not conceited rather I was just amazed about this and I soaked this all up like a very thirsty sponge and was overjoyed that my existence had come to life. I did not question the reasons for this phenomenon. I made good grades, was voted first Chaplain then President of my two sororities, was a cheerleader and was nominated for Miss Borger High School. My parents were still very silent about all this and as long as I made good grades not much of anything was ever discussed or ever even celebrated at all. Mother was wonderful during those years, however, and she let me have slumber parties in our basement and raced through the stores to find nice clothes on sale for me. She let me have Tricia and one of my best bosom buddies, "The Clan", we called ourselves, spend the night at our home anytime we wanted. I'll always remember one of Daddy's bird dogs, Trigger, floppily leaping upon us when we entered the house through the back yard area. He was as tall as we were when he stood on his hind feet and he brought much laughter. All we had to say to one another was, "Trigger!" or "Ignance", another funny pet of mine, and we'd start laughing! I also loved that Daddy always called me and my friends, "Little Engineers", usually when he was paying for our sodas at Barney's Pharmacy. He also always called me 'Catherine Ann'. Both names were very special to me.

Mother and I hardly ever communicated at all. Discussions of any kind ended in an argument so we just didn't discuss anything...period! Mother would have her way or else...no compromises! She once barged into my bedroom where I was sleeping in on a Saturday morning. She frantically woke me up to try on a pair of shoes which she bought me on a half price sale. "Here, Cathie, try these on so I can return them if they don't fit!" Groggily, I sat up and she shoved these olive green, ugly high heeled shoes onto my feet. "Mother, I don't even like these shoes and I don't have anything that color so I have nothing to wear with them," I said. She countered, "They are a good buy and it doesn't matter if you like them or not because you'll never wear them anyway!" And she kept them! And Daddy once bought her a new car and she was so mad at him because she didn't like the man he bought it from that she didn't speak to either of us for several days. Daddy finally told her to take the car back and get what she wanted. She returned with the exact same car in a different color but then she was happy. Things like this I never understood about her...this irrational stubbornness she exhibited at times. She could also be fun and giving and she was a good person but she was not going to be told what to do by anyone. Even suggestions were taken as a personal criticism. As an adult I realized she had been prone to frequent panic attacks which were leftovers from an insecure childhood, I am sure. By this time I had learned to just keep things to myself and to enjoy my own blossoming life and to avoid any confrontations at all costs and in doing so we avoided family closeness other than basic comings and goings. Years later I realized that my parents never came to any of my games when I was a cheerleader in school...a fact that went totally unnoticed by me at the time.

Mother ingeniously teamed up with another mother, Dickie, and I think perhaps Mother knew deep down that she lacked the ability to communicate effectively with me and knew that Dickie would know how. She and Dickie had worked together before either of them were married and Dickie's family had moved closer to us during my junior high school years. This was a great God send to me and Dickie's daughter, Toni, became one of my dearest friends. She has been there for me every step of the way and Darling Dickie would become like a second mother to me and loved as dearly. They drove us to a nearby town on Saturdays to take dance lessons even though we both took ballet and modern jazz at home... with a few piano lessons squeezed in somehow. Darling Dickie and Mother saw to it that we were given the extra polish they wanted us to have. I needed much more than Toni as I was totally into laughing and being silly. I believe that I laughed more during my high school years than all the rest of the years of my life which helped me handle a lot of things in this silence. I admired Dickie very much for a lot of reasons but primarily because Dickie was so outwardly supportive of her children and was a totally involved parent.

Dickie could also accomplish almost anything with her gift of gab. On our numerous shopping trips to Amarillo, we always ended up on a one way street going the wrong way...every single trip! When the policeman pulled them over they talked and talked endlessly about anything and pulled photos of Toni and me out of their wallets and showed them to the officers while pretending to dig for their driver's license and trying to bore the poor man until he was glad to leave them alone...WITHOUT writing them a ticket! Once they actually chewed out a policeman for making them lose the car ahead of them who was supposedly, leading them somewhere! Honestly! They also refused to buy those little nylon foot hose, "footlets" we called them, the shoe stores insisted people wear while trying on shoes. Darling Dickie would say, "Evelyn, let me borrow your nylon hose...I've got a whole drawer full of those dang footlets at home and I'm not going to buy another pair!" Mother would proceed to unroll a nylon hose from her leg and hand it to Dickie who would put it on and try on one shoe and hobble around in one new high heeled shoe and one flat shoe of her own. (This was long before the days of pantyhose.) One of us would give the other the elbow and say, "Don't look now but our Mothers are doing it again!" Although we were dying of embarrassment our Mothers were absolutely wonderful together!

Darling Dickie and Mother handled all the family matters concerning their children without much input form their husbands and together they chaperoned our high school sorority dances at Teen Town. I do believe it was Dickie's voice and great sense of humor and encouragement that helped me to find the "steel magnolia" (borrowed from the movie of the same name) inside me.

When we were fourteen, they let us miss school to go to the Amarillo Airport to see John Fitzgerald Kennedy when he stopped on his campaign trail. I will never forget shaking hands with J.F.K. and holding his hand until he looked directly at me. I don't know why but for some strange reason I wanted to look into his eyes.

My first brush with J.F.K. whose future assassination would have a grave impact not only on our country but, amazingly, on my personal life as well.

~ College Days in the '60's ~

My parents did not include me on any family discussions or decisions nor was I advised to seriously consider what I wanted to do with my life, let alone career. When I was approaching my senior year in high school my Mother suddenly and firmly announced, "you WILL go to college, whether you want to or not, and you can be a teacher, a nurse or a secretary!" as if it were a punishment and I never understood this. When I said I didn't think I wanted to be any of those things Mother replied, "Oh well, it won't matter, you'll be a wife and a mother anyway"... and I believed I would be. (Little did I know at the time that I would eventually do all of those options which led me to become a sort of "jack of all trades master of none", I suppose.) After all, none of the women I knew in my family were career people... not Grandmother, not Mother not my sister-in-law and it never occurred to me to be one either. I simply did not know any other way. Women only worked until their husbands got on their feet, I thought. Daddy told me I should learn to type and that was all of the discussion about planning for my future. I think they believed that it simply was not necessary for females to prepare for a career in those days like it was for the males. Sadly, they never included me on any family discussions... just to describe the silence that always surrounded and engulfed us.

I graduated high school in the Spring of 1965, and in September I went off to the University of Texas in Austin. Forewarned that Freshman English was the big Freshman flunk out course at UT, I took it and College Algebra in summer school at the local junior college. I managed to not make my grades anyway after only a five minute counseling session from my assigned adviser during enrollment with 25,000 students... quite confusing to a new Freshman like me! I ended up dropping Biology, which I loved, because I was told it was impossible to pass without having Chemistry first and ended up in a Geology class with 500 students and a professor who bluntly announced that he did not want to see any of us outside of the classroom and where a grade of 75 was a D. The kicker was that the professor gave us a 25 point major exam question before the exam that never seemed to have the answer he wanted which gave us a 75, or a D, starting out! Anyway, I failed to make my grades. I had not learned to study in school even after taking a tough Biology class in high school and passing with B's. I credit my high school, college level Biology teacher. Mr. Ronald Raff, for being a terrific college-prep teacher and my fifth and sixth grade teachers, Mrs. Bernice Tarver and Mrs. Lois Sublett, all for being the greatest teachers in my life. Had it not been for these three teachers I probably would never have been able to make it through college. My fifth grade teacher assured Mother that I did indeed have a higher than average I.Q. and I saw the look of relief on Mother's face when she heard this. I don't think she never saw much to admire in me.

The first day of classes began with my Philosophy class of 500 students. The professor introduced himself then said, "There is no God!" Then told us to write an essay about that as we read a book by William James for that class. I still had not learned to think for myself, obviously, or I would have dropped that class! And on campus I was practically lost except for my suite mates at a university whose population was the size of my hometown. I had depledged my sorority because they made me date fraternity boys I didn't know while I was dating someone from home, they made me wear a girdle when I only weighed 105 pounds and didn't need one and the sorority house was several miles from my dorm and I had to walk there every night to study in a smoke filled room with 50 other pledges. A date taught me how to drink beer, which I disliked, at fraternity parties by first putting a breath mint in my mouth, then lighting a cigarette, then taking a drink followed quickly by a puff off the cigarette. What a horrible thing to want to learn but I wanted to learn how to "be a big college girl". However, I depledged the sorority within a month or two of pledging. Mother temporarily disowned me over this as if out of the silence I should be able to read her mind! She ripped up the photographs of my pledge week. I still was not being allowed to make any decisions on my own without suffering unexpected consequences for it. This was typical of the communication between us...the great silence followed with a sudden, unexpected fury then by my apology minus any consoling words afterwords which, sadly, was the pattern of our relationship most of her life.

At my dorm, The Madison House, I had six suite mates and half were Jewish. Randy, my roommate was also Jewish, and she and I really hit it off from the start. Together we changed the spelling of our names to end in "ie" instead of "y"...because a "y" bends down and makes a sad ending but an "ie" can be drawn to finish

40

upward...which was very important to us at the time for some strange reason! (My full legal name is not spelled with a "y", so this seemed an easy and obvious change to me.) After classes we liked to watch the most beautiful girl on campus and future movie star, Farrah Fawcett, drink Cokes at the Rexall Drug on the Main Drag or Guadalupe Street. We should have introduced ourselves to her but we just admired her from afar. My roomie worked at Rudy Casual's dress shop, also on the Drag, and was always showing me their latest clothing. Daddy let me write checks on his account but instructed me to put what my purchases were for on the memo line. I found a few things at Rudy's I just had to have and once I actually wrote "equipment" on that line. Daddy never said a word and I feel guilty about that now. Actually, I think he missed a perfect opportunity to teach me how to balance my own checkbook! How I managed to never get overdrawn in my entire life is miraculous! God truly is amazing even about the small details when we ask Him for help. Between God and my girlfriend, Dusty, whose husband was a CPA, may she rest in peace, I always balanced to the penny!

Randy and her parents lived in Austin so we visited her home frequently. They lovingly adopted me and I was invited for the Seder Supper on Friday nights, got to hear her father fervently singing the theme songs from "Fiddler on the Roof" on Saturday mornings and I grew to love and enjoy this close, relaxed family very much. Another life-gift. Her Mom worked in the University Tower and was a published author and her Grandmother, who was also a published writer and poet, was a very delightful woman as well. Her Grandmother rented an apartment within walking distance of the U.T. campus where she audited classes and attended college functions and lectures. She was well into her seventies and she had a heavy Russian accent. She frequently invited us to her apartment for dinner which she always served on her china and silver with no mention what-so-ever of the fast food boxes sitting on the kitchen cabinet as if she had cooked it all herself! (What a fabulous idea!) When we would thank her for a lovely time she always said, "You're so very velcome, my dahlings!" How I loved to hear her warm, wonderful accent and gracious mannerisms! She was an inspiration to everyone she knew and I adored this family and was fortunate they "adopted" me that year and I was honored to be a bridesmaid in Randy's wedding that summer at the Mansion in Austin. They were so intelligent and polished and had close loving and lighthearted families who actually communicated with one another!

Second semester of my Freshman year I met MB in the Dean's office. I was called in and informed that I was flunking Physical Education due to the fact that I had failed to sign up for it and it was a required class for Freshmen. I never knew one could flunk a class for which one was not signed up! This was an omen of things to come in the "red tape and hassles" department of my life. MB and I started chatting and it turned out that he knew a friend of mine, Julee, from Borger. MB knew everyone! We could not walk across campus without at least 20 people stopping to say hello. He was like Barney in that respect. Daddy knew people everywhere we went and so did MB. MB was a fraternity man, a Silver Spur and he had a 3.0 average (UT was on a 3.0 system back then) and was, obviously, highly intelligent. He had a great sense of humor and I really liked him a lot. We began dating and he gave me his Phi Sigma Delta droplet and later he gave me his pin. When I failed to make my grades and had to go to school out of state for my Sophomore year MB and I stayed in touch.

I have to mention the tragic incident that happened on the UTA campus on August 1, 1966, when Charles

43

Whitman went on that shooting rampage from the top of the Tower, which was where my roommate's mother's office was. I was visiting Craig and Cloe at the time when I heard this horrendous news on TV. I called my roommate to make sure she and her Mother and her fiance, who taught classes on campus, were safe and, thank Heavens, they were. Later that month I drove to Austin to be in her wedding and was so sad I couldn't stay for my Sophomore year.

Bless Mother for searching for, and finding, Cottey Women's College, a junior college in Nevada, Missouri. Three hundred and fifty girls from every state and from twelve foreign countries. I nearly cried when I heard it was in a town of 10,000 people, which included the population of the state hospital of 3,000 but I dearly loved it, made good grades and met Karol, a very good friend even today. Karol was very much a life blessing to me. We found each other the very first day at Cottey and we hit it off right away. She was from Arkansas, and our Southern accents matched in a sea of unfamiliar pronunciations and accents. Her dad was a physician and he often sent a private plane to fly us to their home for the week-end. I will never forget his trophy room. It was filled with every kind of stuffed animal one can imagine that he'd hunted himself. In the center was an enormous

44

stuffed Polar Bear. I used to have dreams about that room. Karol and I have stayed in touch all these years. We visited each other's homes during college and since then as well. In 1996, I visited her own lovely home in Little Rock on the way to my nephew's wedding in Memphis, Tennessee. She has a wonderful home with servant's quarters and there is a park nearby called McArthur Park...which brings to mind the special song of the same name..."someone left the cake out in the rain and it took so long to make it and I'll never have that recipe again."

I also made friends with a girl from New Mexico, whose name was the exact name (first and last) as that of my maternal great Grandmother. And, even more surprising, her father was a rancher who bought the Big Country Ranch from Craig's father many years later. (I love it when I can stand back and see that the threads which have formed the tapestry of my life really are engineered by an incredibly wonderful and amazing God. It makes my broken life look purposeful and not as fragmented as it has felt going through it all.)

MB and I stayed in touch the year I was at Cottey then I returned to Austin for summer school, stayed for my Junior year and we resumed our relationship. I managed to make good grades that year but, realizing I would need a minimum of thirty three hours of A's in order to raise my grade point and graduate, I decided to go to West Texas State University in Canyon for my Senior year. (My mother spoke to the Dean of Frank Phillips Junior College about my having changed schools every year and he said it would "broaden my education"...and maybe it did.)

I must mention MB's lovely family all of whom accepted me and made me feel welcome even though I know his parents much preferred a Jewish wife for MB. His Grandparents were philanthropists and benefactors in the far West Texas area. His Grandfather had been deceased many years at that time but I had the great pleasure of meeting his Grandmother, a genuine Grand Dame. She lived in a lovely home with her live in caretaker and MB loved them both dearly. I had the good fortune to dine at her home where I met one of MB's cousins who had survived a prison camp during the war. I will never forget the number tattooed on her forearm. I had always abhorred Nazis but never so much as from then on! During my visits I stayed with his aunt and uncle, MB's Mother's brother, and his wife. I knew absolutely nothing about this or about Mark's wonderful family history until long after he and I became serious. MB had given me no details about them at all. During my visits his uncle would greet us at night coming in from our date and would feed us and tell fascinating stories of his retreat from the Nazis during the war. I wish I had all those visits on tape. I adored MB's Father who was a true gentleman in every respect of the word. He had European manners and actually kissed my hand, opened doors for all women and dressed immaculately. His Mother was truly a lady as well and we soon became good friends. I loved both of his parents! All of his family members were wonderful life gifts and I will forever be blessed for having known them. MB and I became engaged when we were at his home for Easter & Passover in 1969. His Grandmother gave him a beautiful diamond from one of her earrings for my lovely engagement ring, which was so special and I was delighted, of course!

The years just before MB and I became engaged had been preceded by very difficult years for my parents. My Father's younger brother had died suddenly in 1966, followed by my Grandfather's death in 1967. Grandmother was still living at home but she was bed fast. We had twenty-four hour caretakers for her but she was no longer herself which deeply hurt Daddy. Most worrisome of all, in 1967, my brother had thankfully survived a major surgery which concerned us all tremendously. I did not know it at the time but Mother was living under an additional strain as Daddy had begun drinking too much. She protected me from this in her usual strong way and by remaining silent. But MB and I had become engaged and his parents wanted to come and meet my parents. MB was away in the Army Reserves so it would be up to me to entertain and introduce our two families. His family hid their disappointment about my not being Jewish very well. Daddy, however, was not convinced this marriage should take place.

I should explain that Daddy and MB had gotten off to a rough start three summers prior to this when Mark wrote me a letter and addressed it to "Occupant". I think he thought he was being "cool" and in the letter he said he was coming to see me by hitchhiking with a frat brother of his who was going to Colorado to, "see a girl he was screwing around with"… language which my Daddy would not approve nor could he be convinced it meant nothing! Mother always read my mail (always!) and she was mad at me at the time for some reason I don't even recall so she showed MB's letter to Daddy knowing full well I'd be in trouble. Mother usually only told Daddy things when she wanted me punished. Daddy was very old fashioned about things and I thought he was going to come unglued! He grounded me, jumped all over me, told me that if MB came that I was not to see him! I was torn up and MB was on the way! I finally got Mother calmed down and she then agreed to let me see him but she stipulated that he had to stay in the hotel and that I had to hide him and keep him from meeting Daddy or from even coming to our home! After a couple of days Mother ended up feeling ashamed of herself over all for this...after all MB had taken her out for a lovely dinner at the Driskill Hotel in Austin and she knew he was a gentleman and they had been "properly" introduced so she finally agreed to go with me to drive MB to the main highway to hitchhike back to Austin. I managed to convince MB that Daddy would not like his long hair (barely below the ear lobe long) nor his guitar, nor his hitchhiking and hoped that I covered what looked to be like antisemitism which really was NOT antisemitism at all but was concern for his daughter and her "slightly hippie looking" boyfriend...but some people would construe it to be antisemitism especially before they knew and understood my Dad. MB was very adult about it all though and he did meet Daddy that trip and shook his hand and both "boys" acted like gentlemen. MB was totally astounded that anyone would ever think poorly of him because he was from such an outstanding family and had never been rejected by anyone, I'm sure. Needless to say I was extremely embarrassed and humiliated about the entire thing! Are all families this dysfunctional, I wonder? Heaven forbid!

CHAPTER 3

UNDERSTANDING DADDY

M y home town is a small town and lacked having
very many Jewish families and I never thought
much about religious differences of any kind. Daddy
wanted Mother and me to go to whatever church we
wanted and he wanted us to go regularly so we did.
Actually, with the unruly boys I had in my Sunday
School class, it was a thing to be tolerated rather than
enjoyed at least through my junior high school years.

After MB and I became officially engaged Daddy
decided to ask one of his best friends and his wife, who
were Jewish, about mixed marriages. Daddy thought the

world of them and they gave him their honest opinion... that it could work but that it would not be easy and that they'd heard from some mutual friends that MB was somewhat of a nonconformist, which is not unusual with very smart people.

I later realized that Daddy didn't know anything at all about the Jewish religion or their history which I find very endearing because it meant that he couldn't have been antisemitic. Actually, he knew literally nothing other than it was not one of the religions with which he was familiar. Daddy was a good humanitarian and he was not against any people at all! He had close, Jewish friends for whom he had a lot of admiration. He was simply uninformed about this subject. But he was giving the upcoming marriage a lot of thought especially when I told him that MB's parents wanted us to set a date when they could come meet him and Mother. MB had graduated from college and was in basic training for the Army Reserves so I had to handle the introduction by myself. I genuinely liked his parents and I very much wanted things to go well. A date was set and Mother and I were leaving to pick them up at the airport (an hour away) and I asked Daddy to please, please just not mention religion at all and that everything would be fine.

He promised. Mother and I met their plane and everything was going well on the hour long trip home. When we arrived at home Daddy met us dressed in a business suit and we went into the living room for coffee. His parents presented me with a beautiful Lucien Piccard gold and sapphire watch as an engagement present from MB's Grandmother. Such a lovely and treasured gift. I could not have found a more precious family to join anywhere and I truly loved them.

Things were going really well when all of a sudden Daddy glanced out of the living room window and exclaimed, "Say, by the way, we have some Jew neighbors who live across the street! Would you like to meet them?" All of our mouths fell open for a brief silent moment but we all rebounded quickly and they said that yes, they would like to meet them so Daddy went across the street and brought them over and made the introductions and a lovely afternoon ensued. It never occurred to me to tell Daddy that it wasn't nice to call people "Jews" but to say "Jewish" instead. I died a thousand deaths until I was sure that everything smoothed itself over and thanks to his parent's graciousness and to Daddy's genuine effort and innocence about it, it all worked out just fine.

That week-end our family's close friends invited

us to bring MB's family to a Bar-B-Q lunch in Stinnett which was a thirty minute drive from my home. We all got ready to go but Daddy first wanted to give them a grand tour of Borger. Bless his heart, he drove us down 3rd Street, up Main Street, across 10th Street and down Cedar to 3rd street again and he made this rectangular patterned drive more than once in an attempt to make Borger look a little bigger than it was, I think! We all just acted like we didn't notice. Then we were off to Stinnett for the Bar-B-Q! Our hostess was a jovial, genuine and fun loving woman who went out of her way to make everyone comfortable and who would never say or do anything to hurt anyone's feelings...not ever! She had three daughters and a son and her youngest daughter had just married a Jewish boy. (Which Mother had not told me yet.) She greeted us at the Bar-B-Q lunch, and when Mother introduced them to MB's parents, she smiled and gushed, "Oh you must meet my son-in-law...he's a little Jew boy, too!" It helped make Daddy's faux-pas the day before better because with her wonderful smile and genuine spirit, she was very obviously not intending to make any jabs but was simply being her merry, sweet self. Still, I was stunned for a moment there.

We all managed to survive and enjoy the weekend.

The weather turned dark & rainy (an omen, perhaps) and their flight was canceled so they had to stay over another day. "The Night They Raided Minsky's" was showing at the theater and Daddy suggested Mother and I take our guests to the movies Sunday night...which we did. Daddy never, ever went to movies because they always made him fall asleep so Daddy stayed home.

On subjects with which he was unfamiliar, like Judiasm, he did very well, in retrospect. Daddy loved all people ~ period! And although he didn't know better than to use the word, "Jew" instead of "Jewish" it was an honest mistake and he managed to inject his own personality and his own character into a strained situation and to handle it the best way he knew how. Although it could have been a total disaster, it was not, though I couldn't see the humor for many years. Daddy had prevailed and never lost himself in the process! God bless you, dear Daddy. You were 100% genuine and I admire that quality very much.

Things were changing, however, in MB's world. I met him in the mid-sixties and although he was a nonconformist and slightly on the "hippie" side with his longish hair (just below the ear lobe long) and guitar, he still exhibited mostly traditional values at school. He was an active fraternity man, lived in the frat house until his senior year, was a Silver Spur and was clean cut and always nicely dressed. We went to the fraternity parties, formal dances and football games. We even got to ride in an orange and white Cadillac convertible escorting Bevo, the Longhorn mascot, onto the football field before a home game. I never thought he would go any further with that than the black lights and psychedelic posters in his apartment. He never participated in any kind of student protest marches to my knowledge and he was highly intelligent with humanitarian interests that I admired very much. He took me to see Simon & Garfunkel, Bob Dylan, Peter, Paul and Mary and Johnny Mathis on campus and we saw the movie, "The Graduate" several times. He also took me to a sitar concert by the Maharisha but I failed to see the transformation coming up ahead. Someone started the rumor that MB wrote the words to the Simon & Garfunkel song, "I am a Rock", and a disc jockey actually announced that on a popular radio station in Austin. MB went along with it for awhile but it was just all in good fun.

So After MB graduated he joined the Army Reserves and after a few weeks in training he wrote that he'd run into an old friend of his. A few weeks later he wrote 56 that they wanted to try LSD. This really scared me! Many of us students took "dex" or dexadrine occasionally to stay up all night to cram before an exam but I didn't think that it was dangerous or something that was ever used for fun. However, I knew LSD was illegal and dangerous and that it caused genetic deformities and I feared he had gone past the point of return. Prior to this last revelation the wedding date had been set for August and the announcements had been in the newspapers in our respective hometowns. (By amazing coincidence, Craig later told me he saw it in the newspaper.) MB's aunts were buying a complete service for eight of our selected china and crystal and his lovely Grandmother was buying the entire sterling silver service I had chosen. But MB now wanted to live in a Volkswagen Van and to travel around the country after we got married. His parents were calling me asking me to try to talk sense into him and he was calling me and talking about Timothy Leary philosophies almost to the point of constant lecturing. I simply shut down. I could not handle this dichotomy of our two very different worlds and values. All I ever wanted was a home and a family and I did not want to live in a van! I was not a flower child and I didn't even like to go camping! He'd gone over the edge as far as I was concerned. I loved him but my eyes were suddenly being opened widely. I also believe that, deep down, he was not ready for marriage yet, either. College life and married life are two entirely different worlds.

When he got out of basic training in June, MB came to Borger for what would be his last visit before we broke up. Daddy still did not totally approve of the upcoming marriage nor did he know it was about to be called off entirely. MB brought Yogi, the Basset Hound he gave me for my 21st birthday, but Yogi, now full grown, had gotten carsick on the trip. When they arrived late one evening Daddy had already gone to bed for the night. Yogi proceeded to make three large stool piles and one pile of vomit in stepping stone fashion outside Daddy's bedroom door. Daddy heard the commotion and came out to investigate in his boxer shorts, undershirt and bare footed, no less! Poor Daddy managed to step into each and every puddle of yuck that Yogi had made! Repulsed he stormed back to his room yelling, "Catherine Ann, come and clean up this mess immediately!" I made MB do it.

MB was very intense that trip. He was not the same person I knew at all. I actually left him talking to Mother to go to a friend's house for some peace. He was trying to convert us all into becoming strictly vegetarians and trying to get Mother to read a Timothy Leary book. She got so upset she tossed it into the fireplace. He became extremely upset and called this a "book burning, Nazi action" and then he packed up to leave. What a nightmare! I knew it was all over except for the good-bye! I wanted a traditional life, not anything like this, so I was ready for it to be over. I broke off our engagement and returned my lovely engagement ring. He called me again a few weeks later that summer. I was visiting Tricia in Dallas and applying to become an airlines stewardess but I/we had been through entirely too much so we confirmed that we had broken up for good.

Looking back I am very sorry I did not get to have them all as my family. I am glad, however, that I was not the one to deny his Mother a Jewish daughter-in-law and grandchildren. I would have converted without a problem. I was a Christian but was not yet a born again Christian and Messianic Jewish people were practically unheard of back then. Nor did I yet understand the Hebrew roots of Christianity but my heart and soul knew and felt a definite connection. In later years I would learn that I, like all Christians, have a Hebrew Messiah, praise His Holy Name! I've also learned that the very first

Christians were Jewish...that all the Apostles, except for Luke, were Jewish and all the prophets who wrote books of the Bible, except Luke, were Jewish, as well.

MB told me many years later that he did buy his van after all and lived in a commune outside Taos, New Mexico after basic training. He also made a trip to India to study under the Maharisha in person and returned to Texas to build his herb and health food interests into a very successful business. Ultimately he became a professional lecturer and an authority in this field. Ironically, he has been a guest speaker at various Pharmaceutical Association seminars. Ironic because Daddy was a Pharmacist, of course. MB also taught me how to think for myself. He calls me every year on my birthday and I'm very glad that we're still friends. God bless you and yours forever, MB. I loved you and your family and all of you will always be in my heart.

CHAPTER 4

GO WEST, YOUNG LADY!

Daddy sold most of his interest in Barney's Pharmacy in the mid-fifties and bought the Black Hotel across the street where he added two stories and renovated into an office building. He succeeded in establishing a twenty year lease with Phillips Petroleum Company and felt certain he had made the deal of a lifetime. This would have been true except for one thing...inflation. Because inflation was a rarely heard of phenomenon at that time he failed to have an escalation clause in the lease which was a very costly oversight years later. Fortunately, he later bought land and built a large garage which he also leased to Phillips and this time with an escalation clause. (After he died, I found three paid in full, six figure bank notes he had signed all due in six months, staggered out, of course!) This astounds me still! However he would not be making any fortunes again because Daddy's health had begun to suffer. I was 22 years old and had just called off my engagement. I had completed four years of college but lacked another year to finish my degree. That's when Mother told me that Daddy was borrowing money for me to go to college. That's all she had to say.

I immediately applied to Braniff Airlines to become an airline stewardess. They flew me to Dallas for an interview and I was accepted. This was my first very own plan and I was to start training in the fall. Strangely enough I do not recall my parents saying anything about my plan. That summer I went with my parents to our cabin at Pearl Lakes for what would be the last time. Daddy no longer tolerated the high altitude very well and they were going to sell the cabin. I guess they didn't want to worry me because they did not tell me of their plan to sell or I would have first shed many tears (I loved our cabin) and then grabbed the giant, cast iron fish fry skillet which covered all four burners of the original

62

wood stove that had been in the cabin when we bought it. And I would have wanted the photo of the Norman Rockwell print which had hung over my bed that had several thumbnail size scenes I always studied closely every summer since I was a child. Or maybe I wouldn't have even thought of these things back then as I was not focused on material things very much at that time of my life. However I was not asked if I wanted to keep any sentimental momemtos of our summer cabin since I was not told of their plan to sell it. Craig's parents, Cloe and Byce, were at their cabin across the lake with friends from New Mexico. This cheered me up somewhat but I was disappointed that Craig was not along so Cloe issued me an invitation to go home with them to the Diamond Valley Ranch for a few days and I accepted. That decision would change my life immensely!

I had often heard Craig and Wally talk about their ranch... the one they called "The Big Country Ranch" but I had never visited it and didn't really know where it was located. I was visiting their parent's ranch and during my visit Cloe called Craig at his ranch and told him to come home. We rode horses, drove cattle on horseback, went to Ruiodoso, visited Bootsie and had fun for a few days. Then Cloe drove us back to his ranch.

Craig and I were cutting up and pulling pranks on dear Cloe the entire trip. She was such fun to tease and we were just goofing off and I paid absolutely no attention to the passing miles and miles of desert we were driving through. It's very hard for me to understand how I could have missed this but I did. Craig kept me totally distracted and entertained and we laughed the entire two and a half hour trip to The Big Country. That's what I liked so much about Craig. We laughed and cut up all the time and he made me forget problems with laughter with no time for the complicated details of reality!

I recall an incident that really should have knocked some sense into me about him at the time but it didn't. Craig drove me out to a rocky cliff on his parent's ranch to show me Indian Hieroglyphs on some of the higher rocks. It was summer and I had on shorts and sandals not knowing about this climbing jaunt he planned but he always wore jeans and boots. We looked at the hieroglyphs, sat down on a rock and visited awhile. Then when we stood up to leave Craig tossed a rock into the cluster of rocks we were on and the entire cliff began rattling! We were just above a rattlesnake den. I believe he was watching out for them closely, but still! That could have had a horrible outcome. I don't even pretend to be brave about that!

Wally and Craig were partners and owned and lived on the South end of the Big Country Ranch in Southern New Mexico. The brothers worked their farm and Byce had cattle on the North end. On the boy's end there was a small cinder brick house which was their "bunk house". They employed several Hispanic migrant workers who lived in trailers and they farmed feed for their cattle and Craig and his brother went back and forth to help work cattle on both ranches.

Cloe always entertained us very well when I visited. She took us to El Paso and introduced us to her friends there and to Juarez for special lobster dinners at a very nice restaurant. In those days the Pronauf area next to the free bridge was very nice. Cloe spent several days at Big Country entertaining us then she returned to their other ranch but I wanted to stay a bit longer because I was having fun cooking for Wally and Craig and their friend, Timmy, who was helping Craig for the summer. Timmy's folks had a ranch near this one and had apple orchards near Cloudcroft. I had my own room, of course, which I discovered was also home to about five very large and ugly spiders! I exterminated the place and thoroughly cleaned it and then I could relax. Craig was continuously pointing out the positive aspects of living in the country versus living in the city to me.

An example of our silly playfulness: Cloe called the farm a couple of days after she left and I answered the phone and spoke to her awhile then gave the phone to Craig who urgently greeted her with, "Cloe, have you seen Cathie?" She replied, "I thought she was there with you." To which he replied, "No, I haven't seen her in several days!" She then said "Barney and Evelyn are going to be very upset with us when they find out she's missing!" Banter and silly jokes were a constant thing with us. Craig could always make me laugh no matter what I was going through and that's what attracted me to Craig. He always acted like he really liked me and he treated me very well but we were just good friends.

I began thinking more about my plan to live in Dallas and to fly for Braniff Airlines. My only friend in Dallas was Tricia and she already had two roommates. Where would I live? How would I find a roommate? I'd already been a bridesmaid for several of my friends and I was just about the only single "straggler" left. I realized that not only was I ready to get married but I wanted to get married...the time was right in my life for marriage! Then the idea came to me...Mother and Daddy had known Cloe and Byce for many years so if Craig and I married there would certainly be none of the difficult problems I had with my previous engagement. We're all pretty good friends and Craig and I have such good times together...this could work! So I hinted to Craig about marriage and we agreed. We first planned to have a small chapel wedding in my hometown that Christmas but that would not come to be. Instead we eloped in July therefore we saved wedding expenses. The next day we called my parents who were still at the cabin to tell them. None of the cabins had phones so we had to contact Headquarters to send a driver to our cabin to tell them they had a phone call. Mother said Daddy didn't say a word but that tears began rolling down his cheeks. I'd spared Daddy from having to formally "give me away" in marriage something he always said he could never do because he had such a tender heart. We called Byce and Cloe to tell them and Byce only said, "just remember...if you divorce Craig, you're divorcing me, too." I thought what a strange remark that was especially since I didn't even believe in divorce... at least not yet!

As the hot summer months in the desert went by slowly...so very, very slowly reality began to sink in. Where, exactly, did we live? WHERE AM I

ANYWAY??? I got out an atlas and realized, for the first time, that we lived in the absolute middle of nowhere! We were 160 miles East of El Paso, 180 miles West of Carlesbad, 250 miles South of Roswell, and about 150 miles Southeast of Alamogordo, New Mexico. The Big Country Ranch was not far from the White Sands Missile Range where they tested the atom bomb because it was too desolate out there to hurt anyone! Dear God in Heaven, what have I done? How could I ever adjust to this life that Craig loved and that was in his blood?

When I was a little girl I used to look up at the moon and reach out for it and say, "Have it, the moon, Ruth?" to Mother's friend. She would say, "Yes, Cathie, you can have that moon but we'll leave it high up in the sky so no one can take it away from you." Looking back I wonder about these somewhat prophetic words as I would loose everything I had more than once and worst of all that included loved ones...too many precious loved ones who were all yanked away suddenly!

On July 20, 1969, exactly a week from the day we were married, Neil Armstrong took man's first step onto the moon. I will never forget watching this on television from the ranch then going outside to gaze at the moon, then coming back inside to watch all this amazing news live on television, over and over again in total amazement! We could get one television channel if the wind wasn't blowing too hard.

That same day an Hispanic man came through the ranch and stopped at the house. He had actually walked all the way from Mexico City. Craig spoke fluent border Spanish and by talking to him he discovered that this man's parents were the head honchos of Bootsie's ranch. What a small world, indeed! Craig raced into the house and explained all this to me and brought the man in so that he could talk to his father on the phone. In one whale of an unforgettable moment I watched a 35 year old man become totally confused and confounded about this Twentieth Century invention, the telephone. From where I was standing I could see both Neil Armstrong walking around on the surface of the moon on tv and this 35 year old man, who was totally incapable of comprehending the telephone and who could only shake his head "no" while holding the receiver upside down and who never realized his father was waiting on the other end of the line to speak to him. The future and the past were converging before my very eyes all at the same moment in time! This was mind boggling to me!!!

At that moment I also realized that I had married into the past...into a part of the uncivilized Old West.

I wanted to call my friend, Toni, in Houston and say, "Houston, we have a problem!" And I have actually done that very thing more than once over the years.

CHAPTER 5

WELCOME TO MY CAMELOT...
COWBOY STYLE

Mother and Daddy gave us a lovely wedding reception in Borger and I was given a bridal shower at the 6666 Ranch by several of Mother's friends. The managers of the 6666's were good friends of my parents and since I'd married a rancher they thought it seemed appropriate to have my shower on a ranch. I felt most honored. (Some people weren't exactly sure whom I had married due to conflicting newspaper announcements...first that I was engaged to marry MB in August and later that I'd married Craig in July...of the same year...embarrassing and most difficult to explain to say the least.)

The summer was almost over and Timmy would be going back to school in September. Craig's brother, Wally, announced his upcoming marriage to Barbie, who was attending SMU, and they had set a date for the week after the coming Christmas. Wally began renovating the bunk house into their future home. He was tearing down walls, putting in a new kitchen and even hired Charlotte's House of Interior Design in El Paso to help camouflage the place. "Charlotte's Web", I called them, borrowing, of course, from the wonderful children's book by E.B. White.

Barbie was Timmy's second cousin and she was not a country girl either. I was thrilled at the prospect of having a sister-in-law so close to us...just 47 miles away... only to discover that Barbie didn't like Craig very much therefore she didn't like me either. For this reason Craig declined their friendship as he was much too unrefined for her taste (and he was fast becoming so for my tastes, too) but he was genuine...nothing fake about Craig who was more at home on his ranch and with the cattle than with most people. All I wanted was a home and a family with a man who loved me and whom I loved as well.

Craig had a pet pig named "Hot Lunch" that he let come into the bunk house to get tomatoes directly out of the refrigerator...which I stopped right away not wanting a wild pig inside our house! Craig often preferred animals over most people and he knew his cattle very well. I will never forget driving from the ranch to Borger one summer. We passed this enormous feed lot outside Hereford which got his attention. He scrutinized the cattle and then said, "there's one of my cows." I didn't believe him...there were hundreds of cows in that feed lot! He pulled the car over and sure enough his brand was on that cow! Plus he really sort of naturally smelled like cattle! Wild animals usually didn't even run from him. I used to say I thought he was part coyote with no disrespect to his family intended. Craig took it as a compliment, I'm sure.

Since Barbie and Wally were going to live at the remodeled bunk house Craig and I decided to move to the old house at the "J.J.", the pasture at the North end of the ranch. It was another forty seven miles further into more no-where-ness and from the nearest town of Dell, but it had a good sized three bedroom, frame house with a screened in porch around the front. So we moved to this house and began life alone as husband and wife. We busied ourselves with fixing up the house by first deep cleaning then painting it inside and out ourselves.

Only one burner worked on the old stove so we got a new one as a very special wedding present from friends of Byce and Cloe. In order to get the new stove in we had to remove the screen and outside door to the kitchen. That night I saw something flying around in the bedroom and called Craig in to help me get rid of the bird. Craig told me to take a closer look...I first thought maybe it was a mouse because it had ears and mouse like feet but there's no such thing as a flying mouse! No... it was a bat and there were two of them in the house! Visitors from the nearby caverns! We finally got rid of them after we swatted the broom at them for a couple of hours. I should have realized I was in the wrong place for me right then and there but I didn't. The next day I was vacuuming in the kitchen and was using the hose to clean under the cabinets when something stopped up the hose. I turned it off and pulled the hose away and saw a large flesh colored, insect looking leg dangling out of the hose! Heaven only knows what I had sucked up! I broke out into a sweat and carried the vacuum cleaner outside keeping the hose vertical hoping it wouldn't crawl out. When Craig got home I had him clean out the vacuum cleaner but we never found that thing and my skin crawls just thinking about it!

Craig told me about insects out there of which I'd never heard... like the vinegarone. It was supposedly related to the scorpion and when smashed a vinegar like odor was released. And big black bumble bees the size of quarters were abundant. Our very own wildlife collection in our "backyard". In retrospect I greatly regret that I didn't take up wildlife photography on the spot. Unfortunately, the city girl inside me was not yet initiated into the wild to accomplish that or anything else out there, actually.

Dell was now forty seven miles away and had a population of 450 people and less than half spoke English. Trips to the grocery and dry goods store and post office became special events for me. I could not buy fresh milk or meat there so I began making monthly trips to El Paso to drop off dry cleaning and the laundry and get fresh produce and meat which I put on ice for the two hour trip back home. Ice cream was a delicacy if it lasted all the way back. I would shop alone, eat lunch alone and drive home alone...this 160 mile (one way) drive, 60 miles of

75

which was dirt road. I actually saw a bobcat on the road one day. This was truly the wilderness ~ it was eerily silent.

Craig and I had our first big disagreement when he refused to promise to take me to El Paso at least once a month to eat out and to see a movie. Then the problems really began. He knew I was becoming "disenchanted", he called it, with life out there. He was gone most of the day working on the ranch. I sometimes went with him in the pick up truck and sometimes not. The ranch was big and something always needed tending. Byce explained to me how he was able to checker board the acreage with Bureau of Land Management acreage which doubled the size of the ranch and with so little rainfall in this area ranches had to be large to feed very many cattle. I admired Craig's dedication and eagerness to work very hard but we mainly stayed at home and worked the ranch while Wally courted Barbie in style.

I really tried to fit in out there. I even tried swimming in a horse tank with Craig but it was very slimy around the rim and not my idea of a pool. Not to mention that I nearly had a heat stroke getting there in the broiling July heat having traveled in an old 18 wheeler cab with no air conditioning that day. The horses were at his parent's ranch and I wasn't about to get outdoors to garden because Craig warned me of the rattlesnakes.

Craig came in from work one afternoon with a menacing grin on his face which I hadn't really noticed. I walked up to greet him and he just kept grinning then I noticed it...Craig had a long, fat bull snake coiled around his arm with it's head tightly secured in his hand. I didn't know one snake from another and all I could do was jump up and down and scream. I couldn't even move away from him I was so frightened. I didn't think he was so funny anymore and I had great doubts of ever getting used to his world. If Craig had been on my side it would have helped! Byce and Craig both said that life out there was, "tough on women and horses!" Neither of them ever did much at all to help that situation.

When Mother came for her first visit Craig told us he was going to Timmy's ranch and wouldn't be back until the next day. Late that night after we were asleep I heard this tapping noise on the window over my bed. (Remember that I am out in the middle of absolute nowhere!) I looked up and all I could see in the moonlight was the silhouette of a man in a hat standing there looking at me! I screamed and Mother ran into my room and she recognized Craig standing outside my window. He never said a word...he just watched to see what we would do. He thought this was very funny. I did not.

Then Byce moved in with us to oversee the building of a barn. He and his builder lived with us for six months. Byce greeted each day cursing loudly at 5:00 AM loudly grumbling curse words to wake everyone up and he did that the entire time he was inside the house and his hired hand kept spitting toothpick pieces onto my clean floors! Craig was extremely quiet around him and I was exasperated by the whole bunch. During Byce's stay lightening struck our water pump and we were without running water for two weeks. I melted ice cubes to brush my teeth and used a coffee can for a bathroom at night. Then I welcomed a tooth ache and flew home to see my brother, a dentist, as a respite for a few days.

During my visits back home Darling Dickie and Mother became my allies and source of much strength as I related my troubles to them. I didn't even care if I shopped for clothes anymore because all I needed was my jeans. Mother came out there to help me after I kicked my foot through one of the front door's glass window panes! I was trying to kick the door shut to keep the Dingo dog out and my foot went through one of the small glass window panes that covered the door. I was also mad as heck at Craig that day for canceling a trip to El Paso he promised me...but we got to go to El Paso, after all, for several stitches in my foot and some crutches. Mother flew out to help me and bought me a Chinese Pug to help keep me company but I sent her home with Mother because Byce threatened to throw her outside and I was afraid she'd get snake bitten or killed by a coyote or something worse.

The worst thing of all was that Craig was becoming more and more like Byce. I think that he tried so very hard to please his father and all he got was his loud and constant complaining and belittlement all day long. I'm not exaggerating one bit. This was a shocking revelation to me that Craigs's only role model for a husband and father was Byce and yet he was becoming very much like him in many ways even though he feared him and disliked him most of his life, I thought. Cloe tried to help and she visited often and so did my Mother, bless them for this. But I could not make that ranch any closer to civilization than it was and I was about to go stark raving mad out there. I wrote lots of letters back then. My friend, Tricia, said that I needed to hire "Sky Hook" to move the ranch somewhere else. I appreciated the humor. Darling Dickie told me I should leave him but I didn't believe in divorce...at least not yet!

Cloe, may she rest in peace, was concerned that I might leave Craig. I'm pretty sure this is why she drove me to El Paso and bought us a special dinner and we spent the night to get away from the ranch awhile. Before we went to dinner, Cloe gently placed her ermine stole around my shoulders and gave me her mother's diamond ring. The diamond was a gorgeous, white diamond the size of my thumb nail! I knew she was trying to "sweeten my life" so I wouldn't leave, and I love her for that but I gave them both back to her when we got back to our room. Thank the Lord that I instinctively knew to do that. It was the right thing to do.

A friend from Borger returned to the ranch with me after one of my visits home. We made a very carefully detailed map for her husband to follow when he picked her up a week later. I had learned the back roads cut offs on the 250 mile drive from Roswell to our house which saved an hour or more of driving time. I wish I had that map today...it went something like this: turn left at the first cattle guard you come to after the coyote skins on the barbed wire fence on the right, then go 12 miles and turn left at the "Y" in the road, go 35 miles past the post with the cow skull on the left, etc, etc. for two full pages and over a hundred miles. He followed it exactly and arrived safely but the look on his face was priceless after that winding, desolate trip through the desert after dark! He just sat there in his car for awhile with the motor running in front of the house that had suddenly appeared out of nowhere. I think he was in a daze of disbelief! That was a hilarious scene I think I'll always remember!

The next morning Craig got up, went outside and castrated a full grown bull. He had an iron vice like cage which held the bull captive. He came in and threw the bloody things into a pan of boiling butter without even washing them and sat down to eat them for breakfast. My friends were appalled and I was very mad at him for doing that to a full grown bull! I'm sure he was just doing that for the shock value.

Another lifelong friend from Borger, Bobby, and his wife Gail, drove out to see us. We met them in town and then Craig drove him around the farm a bit with all of us sitting in the back of the truck. He thought it would be funny to drive the truck near a poor pig that died weeks before this. I wanted to wring his little neck for that one! I felt fortunate that anyone would come all the way out there to see me/us and I was so mad at him for greeting

81

our guests like that! Bobby & Gail, but thank you for coming to see me! "Friends forever and beyond!". Like we said in school!

The problem was that our home at the "J.J." was on Byce's, not Craig's, land and Byce could come and stay as long as he wanted and as often as he wanted. Cloe said she would buy a new air conditioned tractor and hay bailer for Wally and she would buy us a house. A place in Lubbock called Bob's Custom Homes on Ave Q and Erskine Road built very nice brick custom homes on blocks and we could pick out carpet, draperies, tile, appliances and everything all at the same place. They would build it there and come lay the cement foundation and deliver and place it for a very reasonable price. We selected a piece of land over the hill from the old bunk house, which was now Wally's and Barbie's home, and which was only a few miles from Dell. Back to "civilization" for us! Craig graded a new road to the location and I was so excited about our new home. I think Craig was, too, but he wouldn't admit it. The house had even managed to survive the horrendous tornado in Lubbock that year so it should survive this ranch! The big day finally arrived and our house was coming down the road. As soon as the 18 wheeler truck drove off onto the new road it sunk into the soft dirt and was stuck with still a mile or so to go. Craig had to borrow three or four tractors from neighbors and they drug the truck and house up the hill to the foundation. By sundown our house was in place with miles and miles of creosote brush as our landscape. We did, however, have a spectacular view of Guadalupe Peak from our living room window.

We still lacked electricity, water and telephone lines so I began the work to make arrangements for all of this to be done. The thing was that every time one of the utility workers came onto the ranch to do the work my new sister-in-law would order them "off her property!" Time and time again this happened. Turned out that the only living soul nearby did not want to be the least bit friendly and she put many delays on every single thing we needed to do. Then she and Wally decided to split up their partnership with Craig and me so we had to go sit in the lawyer's office where the lawyer had split everything down the middle with a house on each half. Someone said, "How do we know everything is equal and that Craig isn't getting the better deal?" The lawyer then said, "OK, we'll draw plots out of a hat." My heart sank...I just knew they'd get our new house! Thank Heavens Craig drew the one with our house on it.

I did try to become a part of my surroundings. I was good to Craig's Hispanic employees who called me "La Juerta" which meant the white woman, or so I was told. I also tried to nurse their injuries. One badly burned his arms lighting a gas oven which I cleaned and put new packaged dry wash cloths as sterile wraps on his arms. I was going to use my snake bite kit on one who was bitten by a rattlesnake but Craig insisted on taking him into El Paso for treatment. He had only been scratched by a fang through his boot but he was deathly ill. This was not his first rattlesnake bite which saved his life.

On one of my trips to visit Mother I'd seen our family doctor, and he asked me why I hadn't started a family yet. That planted the seed and I decided I would have many children and that's how I would keep busy. I wanted a big family. Soon after this, Cloe took us and three other family members to Hawaii as a honeymoon trip because we had not had one yet and she'd sent Wally and Barbie to the Bahamas. But it was a couple of months after we met Bootsie in Albuquerque for the State Fair when I was delighted to discover that I was pregnant. Craig just said to Byce, "Well, Cathie's pregnant" as if I'd done it all by myself. I believe that deep down he was just plain scared to tell him.

Craig had built a rock flowerbed around our house and was furious that his dog, Dingo, an Australian Sheep dog, kept digging up his flowers. One morning he got a coyote trap and actually baited it with bacon and left it in the flowerbed without telling me about it. Then he left for parts unknown. About an hour later I heard a horrible yelp. Dingo's leg was caught in this big iron trap and she looked so pitiful. I was eight months pregnant and I did try but I wasn't strong enough to release the trap and I was cautious knowing she might bite out of fear. I brought her some water and called around Dell trying to find Craig. Poor Dingo had to stay like that for hours and I was furious at Craig for being so cruel and especially for baiting the trap with bacon and then leaving. Thankfully Dingo was alright when she was released.

When Craig was sick I nursed him back to health but when I was sick all he did was tell me to go to the doctor 160 miles away without an offer to drive me. Some friend he'd turned out to be! While I was pregnant this total lack of TLC of his remained the same. One night we got into an argument and he told me that if I didn't like it there that I should leave so I had him drive me to Dell to get boxes as I was ready to start packing. I called home and Daddy got on the phone and told Craig he was not going to let me do any packing or moving while I was pregnant and that if he didn't 'straighten up and fly right' until the baby was born he would be here immediately. Amazingly Craig actually listened to him. God Bless you for this, Daddy.

I moved into Cloe's apartment in Roswell a few weeks before the baby came to follow doctor's orders, bless that doctor! Craig made it to town in time for her birth but was upset that he'd had to leave a cow stuck in a cattle guard, about which I was very sorry. At least he made the effort to get there and our beautiful little Leasa, four pounds thirteen ounces arrived in June. I was totally in love with her from the minute I saw her as I think all mothers are. (When I was pregnant I prayed for God to give me a boy only if I was supposed to stay out there because a boy needed a father and the ranch would be tolerable for a boy...but I asked God that if I were supposed to leave him to please let my baby be a little girl. God heard my prayer and I thank Him for my precious daughter every day.) We named her Leasa using this unusual spelling because Craig didn't want people to mispronounce it by saying "Lessa". Later I realized they were my mother's initials with an extra "a" in the middle!

Daddy and Mother came to visit us when Leasa was five weeks old. This was Daddy's first and last visit to the ranch. Mother later told me that Daddy just shook his head and said, "I don't know how she stands it out here." Daddy asked Craig if he would let little Leasa and I return to Borger with them them and we could have Leasa Christened when Craig could come to pick us up. Craig agreed. After the minister Christened Leasa he held her high above his head in his hands for everyone to see. I am so very glad we made that trip because Daddy only lived two more months.

On the car trip back home Craig confessed to me that he'd cheated on me with one of the street girls in town while I was gone. I couldn't believe it. He acted really sorry and he apologized and swore he'd be sweeter to me and try to do all the things a loving husband should do. That lasted about two days then he became his same distant, hard-hearted self again.

A few months later a man from an Interior Design School where I had sent for a correspondence course actually came to my door... all the way out there! I couldn't believe they sent someone in person! (Nor did I realize that my reach for a career would again be thrown off track.) He had just arrived and had started explaining the course to me when my brother called with sad news. Daddy had suddenly died that afternoon at his office. That's when I recalled that the night before I dreamed of Daddy in a casket and I had awakened crying...this was my second 'Pegasus Dream'. I didn't mention the dream to anyone because Mother used to say if you tell your dreams before breakfast they'll come true and I didn't want that to happen...then I'd forgotten about the dream. That was in the Fall of 1971. The next day Craig drove me and Cloe and little Leasa home for the service. I've never seen so many flowers and people at a funeral service. Many people came up to me after the service to tell me that Daddy had given them free medicine or free rent when they came upon hard times. I'm so blessed they told me or I never would have known. My brother and sister-in-law had a lovely dinner at their home for the president of Phillips Petroleum Company and his wife who came as he and daddy were business friends. Daddy was a well loved man, and the pastor from his younger days of whom he thought highly, Rev. James Glenn, came from out of town to officiate read a wonderful poem at his memorial service. The poem was "Abou Ben Adhem", by James Henry Leigh Hunt, and it spoke so well of all that Daddy stood for and believed, especially the part about loving his fellowman.

It wasn't until after I married that Daddy began to talk to me and to treat me like an adult. I think maybe he loved me so much that he thought it was better to be silent than to do or say the wrong thing. How I wish I'd had the good grace to be more like that myself! God Bless you, dear Daddy. I will always love you. (I recently heard that the word "silent" and "listen" are almost the same words and are spelled with the exact same letters.)

I asked Craig many times to see a counselor or minister with me. He refused. He ignored me when I spoke of God and religion (which I should have done before we married but, sadly, I was not yet that wise.) We had an argument one night about the enormous water bill we had on the farm. I said, "Why doesn't Byce pay these bills like he is supposed to?" (Which was his payment arrangement for the farm producing feed for his cattle.) This made him furious and he countered with, "Well, what did YOUR Daddy ever ever do for us?" Daddy had only been gone a few weeks and this hurt me so badly that I slapped him for the first time ever. He grabbed me and turned me over his knee and spanked my bottom with a wooden hair brush very hard so I slapped him again and he did it again. Later, when I looked in the mirror, I saw that my derriere was quite black and blue. That was the first and last time he would hit me. I began making my plans to leave.

Not long after that I found a large rattlesnake extremely close to Leasa's baby pool. Actually, my Mother was visiting and she told me there was a snake in my flowerbed by the front door and I STILL did not SEE it which kept me from panicking and probably from getting bitten!!! Instead I saw a branding iron Craig left in the flowerbed and I thought that's what she had seen so I reached out for the iron and it was stretched out right there... and I almost touched it! I just did not see it but the Lord was watching over me even then because I didn't touch it nor did it strike. I ran out the back door to get the man who was helping Byce drill a water well... with the noise he couldn't hear me until I was yellng in his ear but he killed it with a shovel. Thank Heavens the man was there that day but that really opened my eyes to our reality!

Craig told me that rattlesnakes never came close to people and that they hid in rocks, corners and under wood piles and shrubs but never out in the open like that. This was too much! I thought about how if Leasa were bitten that I would be so panicked I couldn't drive her to the nearest nurse, let alone doctor or clinic that far away, without having a wreck. I could not live like this any longer. I packed some things and we left the next morning for Mother's house. Leasa was only nine months old and I very much regret giving her a 'broken home' and loosing the wonderful friend I once knew but I had lasted three and a half years out there and Craig was no longer a friend. The Lord helped me forgive him and myself for this marriage failure.

A few weeks later he had Timmy call to declare Craig's undying love for me so we made a two day reconciliation attempt. When I realized Craig would never change I called the Mayflower Movers and showed them the way to my house. I only took the baby bed and my clothing but I needed a van to get Mother's piano back to her so I followed the van from Roswell to the ranch, about a 3 hour drive and I stared at the green and yellow image of the Mayflower ship on the back like it was my savior ship taking me back to civilization. To this very day I still absolutely LOVE the sight of a Mayflower Moving Van! It always lifts my spirits! The last one I saw in 2018 was totally white with green letters. I think it might mean I won't be moving any more until I get to go to Heaven! Praise the Lord!

My first big "slamming" was to be by a cowboy but I got myself and my Leasa out of there. I didn't want her growing up out there and I had to leave to keep my sanity. I was the second woman in my family history to be divorced. Divorces were rare during the early seventies and I was glad that Daddy was not having to suffer the stigma of this because of me. Daddy believed marriage was a lifetime commitment... and it is. He was beautifully old fashioned that way.

CHAPTER 6

MY BROKEN HEART

During my divorce my daughter and I lived with my Mother and the first thing I had to do was to make an appointment with Darling Dickie's doctor in Pampa to avoid the embarrassment of facing our family doctor because of my ex's behavior. A friend of Mother's offered to keep Leasa for me which actually saved her life. The day before my appointment I left my car with a service station to have the muffler repaired because it was too low to the ground. When Mother and I got to Pampa, I stopped at a service station and when I got out of the car and I was immediately nauseated and had a horrible headache. The attendant told me the back of my car was as hot as fire then he saw that the repair man had just lifted the muffler and laid the end of it on my bumper instead of repairing it. That caused carbon monoxide to come inside the car from the rear. If Leasa had been with us she would have been in her infant seat on the floor of the back seat. I believe it would have killed a baby in the back seat close to the tail pipe because it made me very sick. I thank the Dear Lord Leasa didn't go with us that day! What a blessing! And thus began my life as a single parent...and everything the devil threw at me. I think it's important to know what Marilyn vos Savant, the lady with the very high I.Q, who writes for Parade Magazine, says when asked about heartbreak. She says, "the medical term is stress cardiomyopathy and may include chest pain and shortness of breath. When a susceptible person is suddenly walloped by a massive amount of stress hormone, part of the heart's main pumping chamber may stretch and weaken. The event is not a classic heart attack but it can stun the heart into malfunctioning and requires medical care promptly. Remember however, Psalms 147:3, KJV, which says, "He healeth the broken hearted and "bindeth up his wounds".

My brother encouraged me to go to Dental Hygiene School. I looked into it but they were full for the next year so I went to Respiratory Therapy school with a friend from home instead. I had to work hard to get used to emergency room scenes and the frequent life and death situations. (I fainted in the elevator after observing a surgery from watching the scrub nurse scrub an open wound really hard and I could actually "feel" it myself, and again after observing my first "Code 99", where a patient had died and the doctor put a needle directly into the heart to administer drugs directly but black, unoxygenated blood spurted out.) Respiratory Therapy had it's own built in problems for a single parent because of having to find week-end and holiday childcare constantly in addition to week-day childcare. Three months into the program I wanted to change my major but Mother absolutely insisted I stay with it so I did. I graduated but ended up leaving the field in order to have week-ends with my daughter. This greatly reduced my earning power over the years but my best and most valuable times were spent with my daughter, Leasa, so I don't regret it.

A year after our divorce was final Cloe called to tell me that Craig had remarried and the girl he married had been reared on a ranch near Fort Worth, Texas and she would, "know how to be happy out there." That comment bothered me a bit but I had met and was falling in love with Kim. Mother called me the following year to tell me that sadly, Craig's wife had taken her life. Craig called me a few weeks later. Kim was there and Craig didn't say much. He never called me nor Leasa again and I believe that is the way he punished me for divorcing him which unfairly hurt her instead of me! His loss entirely! Hurt (adjective) people hurt (verb) people.

My parent's dear friends were EC and BB, and, sadly, BB died following surgery. I will always remember visiting her in the hospital the night before her surgery. She had tried everything to help her painful hip and surgery was the last resort. I realize now that she must have been very frightened about it but she appeared to be her sweet, cheerful self that evening. Before I left she asked me to recite the Twenty Third Psalm out loud with her. I didn't realize I knew it by heart but, with her help, I did. She died a couple of days later. EC was crushed and Mother and I were crushed and everyone who knew her was heartbroken. The world would not be the same without our precious BB.

Several months later EC and Mother began doing a

few things together. It was natural to seem them together as he'd been like family for as long as I can remember. I asked EC to help me meet someone nice. He happened to be on the Hospital Board of Directors and he knew Kim, the Pathologist, who came to Borger in 1968 from Dallas, was single. EC arranged for Kim and I to meet at Mother's house and our first date was a double date with Mother and EC for dinner at the Borger Country Club. (That was the first and last double date I ever had with my mom, but it was a lot of fun.) By the end of the evening I was completely enchanted with Kim.

I was going to school in Amarillo and Kim liked to play golf at the Amarillo Country Club so he started coming over everyday after work and, after golfing, he and I would have dinner together. I soon began cooking at home so Leasa could be with us. I was crazy about Kim, no two ways about it. He was very intelligent and he had a wonderful sense of humor. I liked him immediately and the better I got to know him the more I liked him.

Kim loved to eat at the best restaurants everywhere we went, especially in Dallas. He introduced me to French cuisine and four and five star restaurants. Kim always finished a fine meal with five glasses in front of him...water, coffee, wine, scotch and water and an after dinner liquor...about which I teased him a lot, I also teased him about his face turning red and his ears lying back, just like a horse's ears, when he was getting upset about something. This was my honest observation which, when I told him this, made his face turn red and his ears lie back and he admitted it was true! His son and I had a lot of fun teasing him about this.

We met Tricia, my dear friend from high school, and her husband for a lovely dinner at the Chateaubriand Restaurant in Dallas, where a few years later he proposed to me by slipping my engagement ring in a Champagne Cocktail which I thought that was so romantic. We girls wore long dresses and were prepared for an elegant evening. When the violinist came by our table to ask for a request I could not stop myself from asking, "Do you know "Turkey in the Straw"? First Kim's face turned red, then his ears laid back then he laughed with me. I could not resist embarrassing Kim even if it meant embarrassing myself as well. We had such fun together and I dearly loved teasing Kim...At 6 foot 4 he was like a gentle giant to me. He called elephants, 'efalunts', a rhinoceros was a 'rinocowurst' and a hippopotamus was a 'hippolotomus', etc. He was so very dear to me!

Kim enjoyed snow skiing and staying at the St. Bernard Lodge in the Taos Ski Valley. He wanted to introduce me to the sport but I was strictly a beginner. I'd only skied once with an MYF youth group in high school. My girlfriend, Waynel, and I thought we could talk all night and sleep in during the lessons and then ski on those old fashioned long, wood skis without instruction! We were lucky we didn't break any bones! This time I took lessons and learned to manage the learner's hill which, at Taos, is not a small baby hill at all! I was told that Taos has 3,000 feet of vertical skiing and I just tried not to think about what I was about to do. I focused on the scenery during the forty minute lift ride (two lifts) to the top. I recall my Austrian ski instructor saying, "When we get to ze top of ze mountain you must turn left immediately or else you vill go over ze top of ze mountain!" I'm sure these expert skiers love to tease us beginners when they are forced to ski with us! Honestly! (All I could visualize was the scenes from cartoons where a character goes over this pointed peak!!!) When I got off the lift I turned left so hard my skis kind of stuck into the snow by the ski lift exit and, naturally, I fell. The news that I fell made it down the mountain before I did, of course! I made it down safely but it took me two hours and I was totally exhausted. I did fine on the trails but I couldn't not manage the open mountain very well. Kim threw a party to celebrate that night but I was so exhausted that I took a very not bath and went straight to my room...much too exhausted to eat let alone celebrate!

After I graduated from RT school Kim told me that the nurses at the Borger hospital were trying to unionize and some were walking off the job so they had no one to do respiratory therapy. I talked to the administrator and he hired me on the spot to be the first R.T. department head and to hire and train two girls to work for me. My first full time job. Leasa and I moved to Borger and I worked very hard at this job. There was much to do and I am pleased with the job I did there and I now know to give the Lord all the credit. When Kim came to the Borger hospital their laboratory was in a large closet. So he greatly enlarged and built the first modern hospital lab there and, as the Pathologist, he also served as director over the lab. Hospital Labs and Radiology Departments are the two most definitive diagnostic areas in hospital medicine, I believe.

Our friend and Kim's former pathology partner, V.K., and his wife lived in Pampa and they had us to their home for dinner many times. Now that I was out of school and working I wanted to have them to my home for a special dinner which would be my first time to entertain dinner guests in many years. The day of my dinner party a surgical patient had not come out from under the anesthesia as expected and he was left on the ventilator and was taken to a room on the first floor. The problem was that the entire upstairs of the hospital, including the surgery suites, were on a piped-in oxygen system but only five rooms on the first floor were on the piped-in system and, strangely enough, the plug in systems for the two floors did not match. They had moved this patient on a ventilator into a room without piped-in oxygen and called me to take care of him. This ventilator was actually running off a big green H cylinder of oxygen which is very unusual. I called my former instructor at Amarillo College and asked him how long it would run before the pressure in the tanks would drop and cause a malfunction in the ventilator. He said the tank would only work until it was below half full mark which was about two hours. Darn it!!! Here I was having a special dinner with guests coming from Pampa and I had to run back and forth to the hospital all night long! Leasa spent the night with Mother so I could do all that. Which I did...every two hours...

until finally when the hospital called at 11:00 PM my guests were just leaving, I made Kim go in with me. We finally talked the attending physician, who happened to be there, into understanding why (with Kim's help, thank God) this man must be moved into a room with piped-in oxygen. Each time I changed the tanks it was a race against precious time to change out the tank and keep the patient breathing while I did that by myself! I seriously doubt the doctor would have listened to me without Kim's assistance.

They were actually rolling this patient in his bed with an IV pole, oxygen tank, and ventilator and had about four attendants moving him to a room with piped-in oxygen when it dawned on me! The upstairs oxygen connectors (which fit the ventilator) and the downstairs connectors are not the same and the ventilator is on a tank fitting but we're moving him to a piped-in room. The ventilator would NOT plug into the piped-in oxygen system downstairs at all! Fortunately the Good Lord had actually gone before me because the week before I had just received five oxygen meters that I had ordered and one of these would work in a pinch! I ran upstairs, grabbed a pair of pliers, took the meter off the input valve, ran back down and screwed it into the wall's piped-in system just as they entered the room with the patient! Fortunately, it worked as an adapter but just by about four threads on the screw! Not one nurse or aid offered to help and I was too busy to stop and ask for help! WHEW!!! That was one heck of a close call for me! But it sure did boost my self-confidence which needed boosting as a new graduate. My first taste of pride in a job well done even if it was by the skin of my teeth and even if no one knew what I'd managed to do but me. I was too relieved to even bother trying to explain any of this to anyone...not even to Kim, but all the glory always goes to God who went before me so that I ordered the medical appliance I would need in a few weeks. These are not things one learns in school. It would be a long time before I realized the Lord's perfect timing in everything. When I think about that now it feels like my life has been pretty much hanging by a thread ever since...especially before I realized Jesus was and is always the only Thread Who holds everything together!

I find this particular experience significant in illustrating how vitally important that the attending physician listen to what I was saying but that without Kim's help he very probably would not have listened or even tried to understand the situation. I know this from many other problems I encountered as the "new little Respiratory Therapist". We were considered the 'step-child' of the nursing profession and breaking new territory in a small hospital was extremely difficult to say the least...especially when it involved learning something from me. It seemed as if I were invisible especially when it mattered the most! Yet, more often than not, I was left to clean up the messes resulting from someone's refusal to at least HEAR me. It was very frustrating. I was also chewed out by an ICU physician for extubating his patient when all I did was remove the tube he'd coughed up himself which was still taped to just his chin. I just took the chewing out rather than try to explain as I'd not yet learned to "speak up" to superiors.

Another time the Lord rescued me was early one morning when I'd arrived before all of the rest of the Therapists and the Neonatal ICU (NICU) paged STAT for a therapist to get there. A preemie on a ventilator had extubated himself (removed) his tiny breathing tube which was smaller than a coctail straw, and I was the only other person in house qualified to reintubate him but the anesthesiologist, who was in surgery. I'd observed intubation many times but always on adults as a student, but I'd never seen one done on a premature baby. I was terrified but managed to tube him and before I could secure the tube he pulled it out again! I had to do it all again and I did but all the credit goes to the Lord! I was only His instrument as He guided me. What a blessing!

Gradually, I began to think that Kim had dual personalities and he was a true Gemini, the Twins. At the hospital and in front of nurses and doctors he was totally professional and he wanted me to call him Dr. Kimbell and I did, of course. (These were the days when we were taught to stand when a doctor entered the room out of respect.) He was very easily embarrassed, very conservative and quite old-fashioned in many, many ways...a proper gentleman most of the time and always 100% business at the hospital. But, could he ever "get down" as he called it! I heard many stories about his hot temper but thankfully I never saw him throw a "Donald Duck" fit with credit to Disney Cartoons. I did see him get impossibly rowdy and loud, primarily during football games, which was not surprising. The vast majority of the time he was lots of fun and he was often the life of the party. This side of him began to become more extreme ever so gradually. I think the good Old Panhandle of Texas pretty much destroyed his aristocratic fineness. Of course, I was deeply in love with him by then and I rarely give up on those I love. I knew a very sensitive and warm side of this extremely intelligent and wonderful man. Like an idiot in love I ignored the red flag warnings. True love really can be blind! And I was not yet focused on asking for God's will in my life to be done, and not my own will, other than in the Lord's Prayer, but never asking for His direction in my daily life. What a major mistake that was!

We'd been dating almost two years and I was expecting him to propose to me at any time. We were most compatible and we both were very much in love. I finally brought up the subject of marriage myself. He was very sweet and gentle but firmly told me that marriage just was not for him. He had been married once before and he was absolutely convinced that he was not cut out for marriage. I was heartbroken! I still very much wanted a home and a family for Leasa and me as much as ever and I did truly love him.

Since Kim was not wanting marriage in his future I decided to move to Dallas to establish our lives there. Mother and I took Leasa to Six Flags and I interviewed for and accepted a position there. Craig's Mother, Cloe, came to Borger to see Leasa before we moved even further away from her. I introduced Cloe to Kim that trip. She asked to take Leasa back to Roswell with her for a visit but since Leasa was only three and didn't really know Cloe or anyone else on that side of the family so I agreed but felt I should go, too, so I drove her and Leasa to Roswell. Craig came over to Cloe's house to see Leasa and to introduce his new wife. They had just eloped that week-end. He brought a stuffed animal for Leasa and played with her a bit but he didn't stay long. As he was leaving I said, "Be good to her, Craig, she seems like a very nice person." He replied smugly, "I'm good to all my wives!" This time it was I who was silent...stunned silent!!! Since then they have divorced and remarried more than once, or so I'd heard through the grapevine. But they have remained together all these years as far as I know and I hope they are happy. I really do...I am not vindictive or jealous, and I thank the Lord for that, too.

So Leasa and I moved to Dallas and Tricia helped me find an apartment fairly close to her home. That's when the childcare problems became overwhelming. I worked ten days on and four days off and had to pay for five days of childcare Monday thru Fridays whether she was there or not. I kept Leasa home with me on my days off, of course, but paid to keep her space in daycare those days. And finding and keeping reliable week-end and holiday childcare was a constant problem.

The upside is that Kim's parents and brother and his family lived in Dallas so he started coming to Dallas every week-end to see me. Soon we were back together like before and this made me very happy. Several months later Kim invited me on a special ski trip to Aspen, Colorado, with several friends from Pampa. I decided to move back to Amarillo so Mother could help me with week-end childcare for Leasa and I could go on this trip while I was between jobs. It was on a shopping trip in Aspen that we found Kim's Western style, leather hat and I gave him the nickname, "Mad Hatter", borrowing from Lewis Carrol's Alice's Adventures in Wonderland, again. He loved that hat and wore it with his leather vest and jeans on most of his days off.

It was after the Aspen trip that Kim pulled is first "disappearing act" like his attorney friend used to do. He was a character who supposedly disappeared off a yacht in the middle of the ocean once according to legend... and he was a legend in his own time for sure. And, after knowing him, I believe if anyone could accomplish this feat he certainly could! A confirmed bachelor who owned a house boat called the "SS Not Guilty" which he kept on Lake Meredith. We had a lot of fun on that boat.

Leasa and I were now settled back in Amarillo but Kim had seemingly disappeared and I certainly was not going to chase after him. Suzanne, my childhood friend, called one night and caught me crying. She was living in Scottsdale, Arizona, and she invited Leasa and I out for a visit. She had a daughter near Leasa's age so we flew out for a long week-end and I liked it out there so much I decided to find an apartment and a job and live there for awhile. Bless Mother's heart...she couldn't have wanted us to move to Dallas much less to Arizona but she never once complained about it and she helped us move and get settled. I quickly found a job teaching Respiratory Therapy in a private school in Scottsdale.

In a few weeks Kim called and wanted to come for a visit. Soon he was flying out to visit every week-end. Those were really good times and we loved taking Leasa to eat lunch at a darling place called The Quilted Bear in Scottsdale but soon I realized how very expensive it was for Leasa and me to fly home and back for the holidays. A friend of mine called and asked me if I wanted a job in Dallas working for her boss who owned a home healthcare business. It would be working Monday through Friday, no week-ends, and I was very glad to accept.

It was in Scottsdale, however, that I first faced housing discrimination with apartment complexes where the nicest apartments were reserved only for people without children. The older looking areas were for people with children but were rented at the same price as the nicer ones! I didn't live there, of course! I'd also worked at that teaching position full time hours at part time pay for a few months until I discovered it by accident. They corrected it without apology only when I asked about it!

We moved back to Dallas just before Christmas and I was to start work in January. Mother flew out to Arizona and helped us move. I had not told Kim yet that we were moving back to Dallas because I didn't want him to think I was moving back there just because of him. Fate must have been with me as we bumped into each other at the airport in Dallas flying back to Borger for Christmas and then again when we were on the same flight from Borger to Dallas after Christmas. He asked me and Leasa to meet him in the Braniff Club after the flight and he got my new address. He knocked on my door later that afternoon and we began seeing one another again. He invited me to his parent's anniversary party and he proposed to me that April. I was so happy! My hopes and dreams of a home and a family were finally going to come true. I'd been through so much but this happiness made it all worthwhile. I left my job in July and moved back to Mother's home until the wedding in August.

We wanted to get married at a tiny old mission chapel behind the Bishop's Lodge in Santa Fe but his father was ill and couldn't travel. We decided to get married in his parent's home in Highland Park and, in August, we were married. Leasa was my bridesmaid and Kim's son was his best man. My brother and sister-in-law flew in with Mother and Leasa. I'd been staying the previous week with Tricia. Tricia and her husband, V.K. and his wife and Kim's family and their children were there. I wish my nephews had been there, too. It was a beautiful day. Kim bought a case of Dom Perignon Champagne for the celebration and we flew to Santa Fe and stayed at the La Fonda for our honeymoon.

This was all occurring during the Cullen-Davis murder trial time frame which was the longest, costliest capital murder trial in Texas history, or so I've read. The presiding Judge was a friend of Kim's and every Friday night we joined a group of friends who congregated at Rhett Butler's for happy hour to kick around the latest news. And, for laughs, I'll mention that a well known, now deceased, rancher in Amarillo, who loved building unusual things like the Cadillac Ranch, also built an enormous pool table on the roof of a building across the street from the jail using small bean bags and telephone poles so that the prisoner could enjoy this special view from his jail cell! An outrageous, but true, story.

That summer we spent several days at The Broadmore near Colorado, Springs, with our friends from Amarillo. Our life was wonderful for the most part and Kim was making a very fine husband and father, indeed. I loved watching him teach Leasa, who had just turned six years old, to ride a bike. He was such a dear, wonderful man (especially when he wasn't horsing around and drinking too much with the guys! But most men are like that, I thought as I grew up around adult social drinkers so I was blind to the red flags of early alcoholism.)

Even when Kim was "sipping a few" he handled it so very well that I never really realized he was drinking as much as he was. He insisted on having his UT orange, 32 ounce glass and he mixed his drinks very weakly. At times he reminded me a little bit of Dudley Moore's character in the movie "Arthur", which had not come out until after he was gone but it always makes me shed tears. He was a beloved man who drank a bit too much occasionally but who was happy, fun loving and contagiously lovable…loud and rowdy mainly over football games. Kim often quoted Thoreau saying, "I refuse to live a life of quiet desperation"…and neither quiet nor desperate was he!

I felt very close to Kim. We were heart-to-heart, he and I. This is not to say we meshed every step of the way but we loved one another very much. I had lived alone with Leasa for the past several years and he had been divorced and had lived alone for over eleven years so I wanted to give him his space. So we agreed that he could go to Dallas to visit V.K. or to Amarillo to see his buddies every other week end and I would stay home and spend quality time with Leasa. This seemed to be working out fine for us except that I believe he was either drinking more or couldn't handle it as well but his tendency to totally "over-do" at times was getting worse and more out of hand during his free time weekends. He agreed with me on this and I believe he intended to slow down in this respect but I think perhaps it was no longer under his control. Little boy that he was deep down, he had to prove to his friends that he was most certainly not "hen-pecked" in the least bit now that he was married. And he totally over did everything. There's a bunk house on a ranch owned by one of his friends outside Amarillo named "Kimbell House" in his honor. I didn't go to the dedication because I knew I'd get upset with him and the Amarillo crew and I didn't want to be a kill-joy.

Kim's Amarillo attorney friends always had their annual firm party in November. I usually went to this party with Kim but this time Kim didn't insist I go. Instead he was going to drive a friend's car over to leave at the Amarillo airport for him and then he planned to spend the night at a friend's house after the party. The plan was that Leasa and I were going to drive to Amarillo the next morning and meet him and the contractor of our house for lunch. That night I had sharp pains in my stomach not like anything I'd ever experienced before but I didn't want to be the "little wife" calling her husband home from a party so I didn't call him. How I wish I had because I'm sure now that the pain was a premonition of some kind. Early the next morning my sister-in-law came by for coffee, or so she said, but actually she wanted to be with me when the police officer knocked on my door. The officer didn't know what to say...he asked me if I was Mrs. Kimbell (I said yes thinking Kim probably was in trouble for speeding). Then he said that there had been an accident...then the officer wouldn't say anything else and he just looked down. Then I realized he was telling me something with his silence and his somber expression. I think I said, "He's not dead, is he? Please don't tell me he's dead!" Excruciating silence followed.

That was in mid November...we'd been married only fifteen months and I had to plan his funeral. I was in shock. My friend Toni, Tricia and Rick and V.K. and his wife came and Kim's brother and all of his/our Amarillo friends came. His friends just said, "he was coming home to you." They all assured me he had not had too much to drink when he left the party. I never found out why he decided to return home that night instead of staying over has he had planned to do and it doesn't matter now anyway. I don't really remember much except that on the way to the funeral home to make the arrangements V.K. handed me a scotch and water. Up until that day I couldn't even stand the smell of scotch which was Kim's drink but from that day on when I did have a drink until I stopped drinking entirely, I could drink only scotch with a taste for no other liquor. It was as if even in this small way Kim had become a part of me...he most definitely was a part of me in many important ways as well and he is forever alive in my heart. I thank the Lord I didn't start drinking heavily but I did fall apart. I recall driving really fast to Amarillo thinking, "if life can do this to me I'll give it right back! Thankfully that didn't last long at all and I thank the Lord that Leasa gave me purpose and a reason to go on.

We had his service in my childhood church, the First United Methodist Church, and I'll always remember Dr. Malon Ingham and his sweet wife, Annabelle, singing, "How Great Thou Art" in their wonderful voices and I was sobbing so much I caused their voices to crack at one point. Bless Them. And our friend, Terry, whose husband's car Kim was driving in the crash, gave the eulogy for him from Kahlil Gibran's, "The Prophet". It was perfect, much too perfect for me to paraphrase any of it but it ends saying something like "if we should meet again we shall build another tower in the sky", and the home we were building had a two story, round tower like room in front.

We had another funeral in Dallas. His father asked me to please bring him home to bury him in their family plot and so I did. I'd never before seen fog in the Panhandle but such thick fog set in the next day that his family couldn't fly in from Dallas nor could I see the accident scene between Panhandle and Borger on the way to the airport for the funeral in Dallas. That fog was a blessing at the time but fog now always makes me think of death and of loosing my beloved Kim.

I just *knew* that if only I could get back to our apartment and ask someone to take the pretty memorial flowers friends sent to the hospital (beautiful flowers but reminders of the unthinkable) that I could find him...that this was not actually happening at all. When I finally got back home and convinced everyone that I needed to be alone I cuddled up with his long terrycloth robe that still smelled like him and I cried myself to sleep. That night I had my third 'Pegasus Dream' when I dreamed that he came walking in the door with his right leg in a cast and was his usual jovial self. I went flying into his arms and sat in his lap sobbing that everyone thought he was dead! He laughed and said, "yes, everyone thinks Sid and I are both dead but we are just playing a joke on them." I was so relieved and I was holding him close when suddenly his face turned all swollen and black and blue and I woke up sobbing. A few days later I got the death certificate by mail which said the cause of death was massive injuries to the head and, strangely enough, it stated that he had a broken right ankle...just like in my dream! I believe somehow he reached out to me just as or before he died and I saw all that energy a few days later. I still have very realistic dreams of Kim which feel as if we've actually been together again and I desperately try not to wake up wanting the dreams to never end. He and I were very close and we still walk and talk together in such wonderful dreams I know these 'Pegasus Dreams' are blessings from above.

I'm not sure exactly when I began to realize that he was much more than just a fun loving person...it was almost as if he had a "death wish" the way he pushed himself much too far. After we married I asked his mother if anything traumatic happened in his childhood or if she could enlighten me on his behavior in anyway. She assured me that he had a normal childhood. I knew he had an extremely high I.Q. He told me he could play concert piano at a very young age but that he gave it up at some point. I very much regret very much that I never heard him play. I believe he was a genius, which he very probably was, and I knew most geniuses live and behave in extraordinary fashions. This is how I explained his personality changes from being the most serious physician to becoming the fun loving little

118

boy who drank too much at times. It would be another eighteen years before I was to discover the entire truth.

Kim's favorite poem was "The Jabberwocky" by Lewis Carroll, his favorite author, which he knew by heart. And for a visual art project I made a Tumtum tree and a Jabberwocky and read this poem aloud. I also saw that I was very much like Alice in Lewis Carroll's, "Alice's Adventures in Wonderland"...very lost and struggling to find my way in a world full of so much nonsense that, even though it may rhyme somewhat at times, most things do not make any sense at all! And, even though this is nutty & crazy, I also think Steven Spielburg and I were on the same wave-length about E.T. phoning home. After Kim died I actually thought maybe if I dialed 1-800-+ our 7 digit last name that I might possibly, I know it is beyond absurdly silly of me, but that I might possibly reach or find him...and I tried it more than once. This was before Mr. Spielburg made the movie, "E.T." When I saw the movie it reminded myself of my trying to "call home". I felt so close to Kim that I just knew I could find him somehow! And I did, in my sweet dreams!

The legal nightmare that followed was difficult and lasted over three years. We had not yet made a will...he was 42 and I was 31, so there didn't seem to be a need for a will. (Please, dear readers, if you have children and a spouse you must draw up a will to protect them and yourselves. I've spent lots of time writing, notarizing and updating my will to protect my daughter, dotting all my i's and crossing all the t's.) And the house we were building was under a contract that the loan company had their attorney draw up and we signed together, had it notarized and witnessed in their attorney's office which stated that we would provide interim life insurance fully covering the house during the building period. Kim told them he already had two life insurance policies in his lock box that he would bring these to the mortgage company for this specific purpose. But whomever Kim gave them to at the savings and loan failed to have him sign a beneficiary change (which was still in his ex-wife's name even though they divorced over eleven years before we married which was logical as long as he was single to have her as beneficiary especially when their child was still a minor, and his son had a policy by himself.) But I also know that was never Kim's intention to leave it in her name after we married and his actions showed his intentions about this beyond a doubt.

Unfortunately our copy of the contract was in his

briefcase and was destroyed in the accident but when I asked the attorney who drew it up about this contract, he just said, "What contract?" Much later I found his bill for that contract...which was my only proof it ever existed. After the accident the personnel lady at the hospital where Kim worked, called me herself and told me that Kim told her to make me the beneficiary on his life insurance policy there but she changed jobs within the hospital and never did it.

I was told later that the day of the funeral in Dallas our banker, to whom I thank for this, asked an involved professional whether to let two large, five figure investment checks which Kim had written the day before he died, to go through or not and he advised him to let them go through without even telling me about it. That investment was a total loss. I'm sure he wanted what he thought was best for us but that was not the time to gamble on an oil well investment especially when neither of us needed enormous drilling costs. It was worth very little.

I had a good attorney but he didn't realize he could advise me to claim Kim's intentions regarding the policies legally and I didn't know I could until it was too late, so the vultures prevailed! I am not a sue-happy person and I have let more than one potentially large lawsuit pass to avoid the grief. I was a woman alone with no father and no husband to stand up for me and this was like an engraved invitation to the world to take full advantage! I never would have imagined this could happen until I lived through it myself.

I know Daddy would have turned over in his grave to know how I was treated by his fellow Borgans! He loved Borger and served it well for many years and was well respected and highly thought of person. That didn't matter one ounce after he was gone! My brother came by house everyday after work to visit for awhile and I will always appreciate that but no one could help or console me. The house, which the builder promised to be done by Thanksgiving was only 1/4 completed. I must mention one of the most honest and honorable men I've ever met, Mr. J. Tiner, and may God bless him where ever he may be. He showed up totally unexpectedly at my house and paid me for Kim's half of a very good quarter horse they owned together. I'd never have thought to ask about it had he not come on his own. He put everyone else to shame that I had to deal with. I've forgiven everyone involved because the Lord says we must so we can be forgiven. All of these things were horrible enough but the main thing was that I had lost my beloved Kim. I was only 31 years old and I had to bury my husband.

Our friends in Borger and Amarillo were mostly couples and so I felt like a "third wheel" so to speak. I still had friends in Dallas and so I decided to return there after the school year ended for Leasa. My injured heart was bleeding and I was very grateful I had my precious Leasa, my reason to carry on. I went to UT Dallas to finish my Bachelor's Degree going to school full time and handling these never-ending legal issues and this great and consuming grief. My only pleasure in life was my precious little Leasa. Being a single parent is very difficult but she literally saved my life. I began studying a lot of spiritual readings, I prayed a lot, and believed I was slowly healing my broken heart. Sadly, I was not reading the Bible but reading primarily Christian literature. Suzanne, my childhood friend, also moved to Dallas from Arizona the same month I moved back to Dallas. (Another life blessing!) She lived in her brother's house out in the country on ten acres close to Frisco and across the road from the place they filmed "Dallas", the weekly tv show and back when Frisco had only one Dairy Queen. Leasa and I spent many week-ends out there with her and her children. I was very grateful for this peaceful get away from the city.

In August, 1981, I graduated Cum Laude with a B.A. in Visual Arts. I applied for teaching positions at all the surrounding schools but did not find an opening so I fell back on my medical background and was hired that month by Texas Neurological Institute in Dallas to work as a medical secretary and photographer for Dr. S., a Neuroradiologist and the Medical Director of the Radiology Department at Medical City Hospital. I liked this job very much and it turned out to be my favorite job of all. Dr. S. was a jewel to work for. He taught me how to put up all the angiogram X rays in a specific order onto a lighted, fifty row, rolling screen so he could read them and dictate his findings. He taught me to do the same thing for all the CT scans and how to photograph these X rays for medical lectures and articles he and his group frequently made. I also got to video some of his TMJ fleuroscopy procedures and I made slides of printed material for their lectures. He even helped me with detailed instructions on making a camera out of an oatmeal box for a science fair project for Leasa for which she won a first prize in her fourth grade class. He was a superb teacher and a friend as well as a boss to whom I will always be grateful and will remember fondly. A major life gift for sure. The reason I left this job was because Leasa would be in college soon so I believed I needed to make more money and I believed I could do that in real estate. Another major mistake also made without prayer!

Each one my single girlfriends in Dallas moved away for one reason or another. Of course, I was still grieving over Kim. Now that Craig had a wife she invited Leasa to visit them in Dell and to meet her new half-brother, Bice, when she was eight years old. She also sent Leasa school clothes and birthday and Christmas presents for a little while and I was so happy for Leasa about their efforts to reach out to her but this stopped forever when they separated the first time. He has not seen or contacted Leasa since that visit. He never missed a child support check but I can hardly forgive Craig for ignoring Leasa like he did. Cloe died before Kim and I were married but if Cloe had lived she never would have allowed this total estrangement. Cloe loved Leasa dearly. I have always felt so badly for giving Leasa such a absent father! He treated me like royalty before we married so I failed to foresee his potential to be very hard hearted! I've now learned that women need to study closely how a man treats his mother and how his father and he interact to get a glimpse into her future with him if they marry.

I made a trip to Las Vegas worth mentioning. Leasa was little and Mother came to stay with her while I went with friends. I was getting out of a hotel limousine in front of the Golden Nugget when I noticed a most unusual looking man on the front steps. He was wearing a gray tuxedo with a matching Stetson hat and he had a blonde handlebar mustache. I thought to myself that he looked like a character out of a painting. As I walked up the steps and got closer to him I noticed he was looking at me out of the corner of his eyes...staring at me and that's when I realized it was Craig! I walked over to him and tried to hug him...after all this was my life-long friend from childhood, my former husband, and the father of my child...but then he wouldn't even look at me nor did he speak one word to me. About that time his wife came walking up and said hello and asked me all about Leasa. They were there to be remarried. I find it rather odd that the first two times they married I saw them the next day!

After Leasa graduated from high school I took her to see Dell. I wanted her to actually see it for herself as a mature young lady. We visited Byce and the ranch and he drove us up to mine and Craig's former home. I couldn't believe the difference. Craig had planted so many trees it looked like the house was in an orchard. It was much prettier than I imagined it could ever be. Sadly, I'd heard that Wally's wife, Barbie, had suddenly died of a stroke. I also knew that Craig and his third wife had divorced and remarried more than once. Craig left to visit Bootsie when he found out we were coming. I was not surprised. Craig always said, "You left me and you know where to find me if you want me." Sadly he applied this to Leasa as well as to me. I tried very hard to help her understand that he was trying to punish me, not her, and that his hard hearted ways were not entirely his own fault but was due to his own abusive father. The purpose of this trip was to help her see the place I believed I had to remove her from as a baby to spare her a tough life in a remote place and to see that I had to leave to maintain my sanity. But the cost was dear...it cost her a father and every child needs a father. Craig has not seen nor contacted Leasa since she was eight years old. I think God has a special plan for fathers who are complete no-shows! I did learn, however, that even very good friends need to be very much in love and they must involve the Lord in their daily lives if they are committed to making a marriage last forever. It is hard to see how such a good person as Leasa could be born from our marriage and I thank God for her every day. She and I had no mother/daughter problems until just before she began college.

The lesson here is that our earthly fathers can and do hurt us badly...and hurting people hurt other people so it becomes a vicious cycle...UNTIL we put our Heavenly Father first...then everything else will finally fall into place! It is very clear to me now that I should have asked God to show me His will, and not mine, before I married Craig, for sure, and even Kim, but I STILL had not learned know to do that except in the Lord's Prayer. By not daily asking for His guidance and His will, also for not seeking His Will in His Word diligently, I paid a very high price. In fact, I ruined my life before I found Jesus and His mercy, forgiveness, and daily guidance. Praise His Holy Name!

Kim used to jokingly tell me that if he were an animal he would be a brown bear and that's what he named his brown Jaguar, "Brown Bear". Before Kim and I were married I began calling him Papa Bear and I was Mama Bear, and, of course, Leasa was Baby Bear. Fast forward to the summer of 2009.

My friend, Cathy, has a cabin high up in the trees between Eagle's Nest and Angel Fire. I liked to sleep on the couch in her living room at night and the couch backed up to the wall of the living room. I was sleeping soundly when I heard something walking around outside just next to the wall where I was sleeping. I could tell it wasn't a deer because it didn't have hooves and I turned on the outside light but the light just went straight into the back yard and not to the side of the house at all. Then later that night I heard soft snoring through the wall and it sounded like he was lying right next to me. The next morning I told Cathy I thought I'd slept next to a bear but she swore they'd never seen one in the area for all those thirty some odd years she'd owned the cabin. I still believed it was a bear. That morning she and I got dressed and drove into Taos for lunch and shopping. When we got back to her cabin that brown bear was on the front porch as if waiting for us to return! We waited for him to go around the side of the cabin and then we made a run for the door (which was down the hill a ways and not right next to the driveway.) Then we went out on her back balcony and talked to him and he charged at us. He eventually wandered off deeper into the trees but now I know that I slept with a bear right next to me...and I like to think it might have been Kim's spirit...but not really because

I'm a Christian however he would love that story. I must remember to tell him when I see him again.

With Kim, I didn't believe in giving up on someone I love and I followed my heart again. God bless Kim. I miss him still and I'm sure I always will.

The movie, "The Family Man", reminds me so much of Kim and myself in so many ways that I know he was speaking to me from Heaven in the movie because of the overwhelming parallels in our life. So much that I must include examples here: (My dear friend, Mike Hanner, bought me the DVD of this movie as a gift. Thanks, MJ! I call him my 'Great and Wonderful Sage' because he has helped advise me on many things over the years. And thanks, Mike and Sandy for adopting me into your family.)

* Jack Campbell - Kim Kimbell – main character's name.
* Kate Campbell – Kate is short for Katherine, my name is Catherine.
* Nicholas Cage looks a lot like Kim – same nose, ears, mouth, face shape but different color of hair.

* As a bachelor Jack lived in a high rise apt in NYC – Kim had a high rise apt on Turtle creek in Dallas for several years.
* Jack was an entrepreneur stock broker & Kim had similar side interests.
* Jack's client's name was Bob Thomas – I had a co-worker at neighboring hospital with same name.
* Jack was to fly to Aspen and Kim and I went to Aspen with several friends.
* Main story was about a successful NYC stockbroker bachelor vs being a happily married family man which is very similar to Kim's life & I believe this movie is a message from Kim to let me know he was happy being married to me.
* Jack used the word "superb", as did Kim.
* Jack drove a Ferrari; Kim drove a Jaguar.
* There was a round spritzer bottle at Jack's friend's house exactly like Kim's & I've never seen anywhere else.
* A bicycle bell was the magic signal in the movie and in spelling his last name he always said, " KimbEll not KimbAll as we ring we don't roll".

* Kate used the word, "annyhoo", for anyhow, and my dear, friend and 2nd mother, Dickie was the only other person I've ever heard use this word *ever* so I *knew* again, Heaven was speaking to me!

* The expensive green suit Jack wanted to buy in the movie was identical to the green suit Kim wore at our wedding at his parents home.

* Evelyn was the name of another character which was my Mother's name.

* Roses played a part in a dinner scene at a lovely restaurant like the ones Kim and I enjoyed.

* Annie, their daughter rode her little tricycle and Kim taught Leasa to ride a bike and he played in the snow with her like in the movie. Also, Ann is my middle name.

* A company named "Med Tech" was in the movie and Kim was a medical doctor and I was a Respiratory Therapist or a "Med Tech".

* Kate had a small brown file box with Jack's things in it from college and I had an identical box like that but one doesn't see them anymore.

* Kate wore a camel coat in the last scenes and, sadly, I buried Kim in his new camel jacket.

* In the final scene they are drinking coffee in the airport against a midnight blue sky just like the one we drove under as we arrived at Eagles Nest Lake, NM, which was covered in snow under a full moon. The most beautiful scene ever!

This movie was made in 2000, and Kim died in 1978. I still have the most realistic dreams of him and every time I watch this movie and see the similarities of Kim's face in the actor's face, I shed a few tears but I also love this movie so much as it was a gift from Heaven to me, from Kim and the Lord, and I have no doubt that it was full of happy messages to let me know that Kim, like Jack Campbell, preferred the family life with me over the bachelor life he'd lived for so long before we married. And that even through death that love overcomes and I thank the Lord for this healing gift!

Many people think I am forever 'stuck in the past' but when I write about Kim and how I came through it all I am giving my testimony about the Lord as well as honoring Kim and his memory. I recently found this article in Oprah Magazine, November of 2016, saying researchers believe that being nostalgic may actually make us happier and healthier. Psychologist, Constantine

Seikides, PHD, of the University of Southampton in England extensively researched the effects of nostalgia in an article in "Trends in Cognitive Sciences" and said, "fond memories can generate feelings of engagement and self esteem that leave us more optimistic, inspired and creative."

CHAPTER 7

AND THE INDIANS

A few months after I lost Kim I signed up for an oil painting class at the college and I painted an Indian chief. A lot of grief and many tears are in those brushstrokes. I still wonder if this was a premonition to a friend of American Indian descent entering my life five years down the road.

I worked full time in Dallas and Leasa spent her summers in Borger with Mother. (My parents were very strict with me when I was growing up so I assumed that Mother would be watchful over Leasa. I was quite wrong but that's another story.) I always dreaded letting her go for the entire summer and was so happy when she returned. I pretty much worked my job, loved being a mother and was a single parent home maker. Within a couple of years my closest, single girlfriends in Dallas married and moved to Houston and New York, respectively, and Tricia was already married so I was left to find my way alone, yet again. I very rarely went to happy hours and I was not into bar scenes or single groups. Prompted by friends I did eventually join a single's club but I only went to one meeting where the men sat on one side of the room and the women on the other which reminded me of junior high school and I quickly lost interest. I've never enjoyed dating very much unless it was with someone special or a double date with friends.

I had a secret crush on "Cousin Will", I called him, a Harrison Ford look alike and friend, who took me to the loveliest private parties in Dallas I'd ever seen. I had a crush on him but I didn't call guys and we remained just friends. I never actually set out to search for a special fellow or husband. I believed that if it was meant to be it would be, "Que Sera, Sera", like the song Doris Day sang. It is extremely difficult to make friends and to find one's place in a society built around couples especially in a man's world like it was in the late 70's and 80's (and now, too, in many places) and very few women my age were widowed so young or were even still single. As a dedicated single parent working full time I just didn't find many opportunities to meet other singles and I've always been pretty much of a home body.

In the summer of 1982, a girlfriend I worked with and a friend of hers invited me to happy hour after work and I went. I had not been to a happy hour in many years. That's when I met a man (who later told me he was of American Indian descent) who was quite handsome, clean cut, well dressed and appeared to be and acted very much like a gentleman. He kept looking my way then he came over and introduced himself to us then his group joined ours and they kept the bloody Mary's coming much too long. Looking back I think the fact that a few people I knew were there made me feel safer somehow, in this big city full of strangers.

I want to be clear that I have been blessed to have several friends, and even a most special family member, who are of American Indian heritage and I've enjoyed their friendship and admired their painting, sculpture, weaving, jewelry, history, and every aspect of their culture and have decorated my homes with their art all my life. And the same is true of Cowboys. I love my Western heritage and I believe there are no better people than those with genuine Cowboy and/or Western histories and hearts! When I was growing up many movies had Cowboy and Indian themes which made a catchy, coincidental title for my book but has nothing whatsoever to do with race.

All I am going to say about this person is that he was a very charming man who turned out to be a "wolf in sheep's clothing". Matthew 7:15, KJV, "Beware of false prophets which come to you in sheep's clothing, but inwardly they are ravening wolves." I also learned that the devil doesn't *ever* usually look like a devil and he can, through disguises, get into our minds quickly unless we have protected ourselves by knowing and following His Holy Word in the Bible. What I thought was a blessing very, very gradually became a controlling mind game that bordered on being scary. Again, my lack of asking for God's will in all situations had been missing in my life and so allowed unwanted consequences.

Looking back there were numerous 'good old boys who stood against single women like me, single whether we wanted to be or not. We were treated like nobodies unless we were married to someone, just because they

138

could. Didn't anyone know what the Bible says about how to treat widows and about the Golden Rule? My Daddy would turn over in his grave, God rest his soul, if he knew what his fellow businessmen in our hometown did to me to cover their own errors. Only with the great grace and love of God could I come through everything with my sanity...thus the birth of the title of this book, "Cowboys and Indians and Pegasus Dreams", and as I said before, Pegasus represents Jesus on a white horse literally saving my life. Revelations 19:11, KJV. Praise our Precious Lord!

Meanwhile, the years were flying by and I was working full time. I was mother, father, bookkeeper, house keeper, decorator, insurance and vehicle handler, problem solver and, in other words, I had to do everything that needed to be done or it didn't get done at all. I handled things very well with the exception of making a plan for my life which I still can't seem to do! The legal issues alone were unending. Only a single parent knows what it is like to handle everything alone. It is daunting and almost impossible to do effectively and this was before I knew I could ask for Jesus' help with everything in life. I once read an article in the Dallas newspaper by Dr. James Dobson, founder of Focus on the Family, who said that being a single parent is a "Herculean task" and I felt a warm rush of appreciation wash over me as I read that because no one ever noticed my efforts, let alone complimented me on them! I did feel like I was Hercules who held the entire world on his shoulders especially before I was a born again Christian and knew to give my problems over to Him daily.

Our frequent visits to Toni's lovely home in Houston were special trips for us and Leasa and I spent several Easter holidays there. She and her husband were like an extended family for Leasa much like my parent's friends had been for me. Had it not been for Toni, Leasa would have grown up thinking most people live in apartments and struggle to juggle all the business of life alone. They always entertained us royally and took us to very special cultural events and restaurants. They even treated us to dinner at The Mansion in Dallas when it first opened and to the play, "The Best Little Whorehouse in Texas". I thank them for acting as our surrogate family many, many times. Toni has been my touchstone for my former life before my life struggles began.

In the mid-eighties, I left my job at Medical City Hospital to get my real estate license thinking that with a daughter approaching college age I needed to enter a field with more potential income. I soon regretted that as I really loved that job and it proved to be very poor timing on my part. The real estate office I joined in Plano closed after a few months and I had a difficult time finding another job so I worked for a temporary agency for awhile. While we were visiting Mother a couple of years later, I applied for a position at a hospital as an employment recruiter and I was hired. We moved to the Panhandle in July, and my new job began that summer. Leasa had just finished her Sophomore year, a difficult time to move a child, but she was wonderful about it as she was a precious and cooperative daughter. At that time she was taking driver's education and was learning to drive on Central Expressway in Dallas. That in itself was reason enough to move as far as I was concerned!

Then my brother told me about a great townhouse which was reduced in price due to a bank foreclosure and I suddenly owned my first home. Finally, after all these years, I owned a home of my own but it was too late because Leasa graduated from high school just before I bought it and she never lived there with me. In fact, she only spent one night there with me when she had her tonsils taken out. Life had cheated us again!

Sadly, my Mother began to seriously interfere in a

most negative manner. When Leasa graduated from high school Mother told her she would send her to college anywhere she wanted (within reason, of course) and that she did not need to have my permission nor my approval. I honestly believe that was Mother's way of punishing me for not having married again. Although I tremendously appreciated her sending Leasa to college she was leaving me entirely out of the picture again and was giving Leasa far too much freedom for her age and there was absolutely nothing I could do about it. There were one or two difficult scenes between us and if it hadn't been for Darling Dickie and Toni I would have lost my mind with frustration. They affirmed my very being whereas my mother seemed only to negate it. Leasa was the one thing in my life I was determined to do right and so far I had managed to bring her up without duplicating my Mother's silent and difficult ways which had been a major goal of mine. My brother even tried to help me talk some sense into Mother's mind but no one, absolutely no one could tell my Mother what to do...or even make a suggestion. Leasa decided to go to Frank Phillips Junior College and first lived with Mother, then she wanted to move to an apartment there. We tried to help Mother realize that no one allows their 18 year old daughter or granddaughter to live in an apartment in Borger...that they either live at home or in a dorm...but she wouldn't listen to us and allowed Leasa to move into an apartment which was a big mistake. Leasa had a rough first year of college until I withdrew her while passing and a dear friend of mine and Kim's, Dr. Harvey, gave her a job in his office until her second year of college began at WTAMU. Mother's interference created a gulf between Leasa and me that has been very difficult to bridge over the years. Leasa graduated with a major in Computer Science and a minor in Engineering. I am so proud of her and very grateful to my Mother for her college education in spite of extreme difficulties Mother gave me.

All of my friends had been married for several years and most of them were into their second and third homes and were taking special vacations with their families. My vacation time was spent at Mother's helping her to maintain her home and I was happy to help her the only way I could. But I was spiffing up and decorating and just getting older. She had developed cataracts and could not see very well until they were removed and her maid took full advantage of this. If she even swiped through the middle of the house I couldn't tell it. I could not stand to see her lovely home in a state of semi-disrepair so I took it upon myself to spiff it back up and refurbish everything during my frequent visits home. Mother first took this as an insult and so I had to do much of my spiffing up at night after she had gone to bed but do it I did. I took every single room and tended to repairs for this two level fairly large home until it shined once again. I tackled the dandelion problem in the yard which had spread since the yard man insisted on merely mowing over the weeds. The task was enormous but I was determined not to let the property go downhill and I was doing it for myself as well as for Mother. Being there only on weekends left me no time to find a housekeeper to help me. Eventually, Mother came to appreciate it, I think, but not at the time. I just kept on "keeping on". I was too busy to even think straight most of the time as I was just going from chore to chore like a robot...whether I was at her home or at mine or at work.

I was working my full time job at the hospital which had become more and more demanding and which had a giant, built-in problem: they had given me no credit for my past eight years of medical experience when they hired me at the bottom of my salary scale yet I had to tell applicants every day that "yes, we give credit for past related experience at approximately 2% per year above minimum starting salary. As a therapist I had worked in almost every area of a hospital and I'd even been a hospital department head and I had at least five years of previous work related experience! I was also married to a Pathologist and understood how a lab worked but I didn't include that in my calculations. They did increase my job class one level when they hired me but I was still hired at minimum starting salary for that job class and I was ignored every time when I asked them about this before each annual review. When they told me five years later that I would be assuming the Nurse Recruiter's job on top of my own hectic job and at no extra pay (when the Nurse Recruiter had been making double my salary) including my doing nationwide advertising and phone communications for applicants for the Director of Nursing position myself, I gave up. I wrote three letters of resignation, one for the President and Vice President of Human Resources and one for the hospital CEO, which I made effective immediately. I said I would work a two week notice if they would ask me but they didn't ask. I can still recall the huge black clouds that were forming as I left the hospital and it rained for a whole week after that and I slept that entire week. I had been, I believe, "right as rain" about the situation. I believed I was right, rather, I KNEW I was right. After five years of my requesting every year to meet with them about this prior to my annual review and being totally ignored, I left. I recalled Dr. S. saying, "To thine own self be true", quoting Shakespeare, and I've fought very hard to do this many times over the years.

~ When I Prayed to Die ~

With the exception of the years surrounding Kim's death the next several years were to become the most difficult years I ever endured. So much sadness beyond my control began occurring that I thought my heart would finally, actually break into pieces. First, Darling Dickie died in April 1991. In February of 1993, my dear brother died tragically. I was heartbroken, as we all were. At his memorial service the pastor read I Corinthians 13: 4-8, NKJV, which exemplifies my brother very well saying, "Love suffers long and is kind; love does not envy, does not parade itself, is not puffed up, does not behave rudely, does not seek it's own, thinks no evil; does not rejoice in iniquity but rejoices in the truth, bears all things, believes all things, hopes all things, endures all things and love never fails." Even in his death he was defining love for me and when I returned home after his funeral I had a letter he'd written to me and mailed before he died. He was a beloved man and he is sorely missed by many including by me. I loved him very much and I will always miss him. I light a candle on his birthday and on the day he died every year. John 15:13, KJV, says, "Greater love has no man than this, that a man give up his life for his friends." This makes me think of him.

My Mother's health went downhill very quickly after my brother's death but I believe she did begin to finally to see me as an individual person for the first time before she died two years later. I had begun going to see her every weekend to be sure she was alright. It seemed that suddenly she had become a sweet little old lady in a rocking chair and I would listen to her whispering voice for hours because I knew a day was soon coming when I could no longer hear her voice. She began falling and hurting herself badly and when we thought she was going to have to have surgery on her arm from a fall she gave me full power of attorney (thanks to a family friend and attorney who was helping me with another legal issue) just a few months before I would have to use it to insist that she move to Amarillo to a private home with 24 hour care. I hated to do it but it couldn't be delayed any longer...to wait any longer would have been neglectful of me. She could no longer manage to care for herself at home and my house had three bedrooms but they were all upstairs and she couldn't handle stairs. I found a private nursing home that took only three patients in each home and I felt good about that. It was the best I could do for her and I felt very fortunate to have this option. She died only six months later in February of 1995. I loved my mother very much in spite of everything, may she rest in peace.

The Lord was watching over me because I was so busy working my full time job and then moving Mother and taking care of her home trying to get it ready to sell that the months passed by like hours. She had kept everything during the forty six years she lived in her home and there were so many memories and so many things to sort through and the beautiful antiques and special things that I had no room to keep that I didn't want to go to storage so I hired an antique dealer to do an estate sale. I would rather have her things lovingly cared for and enjoyed in someone else's home than to be locked up in a dark storage bin. I couldn't bring myself to go to the sale and mother was in the hospital during this time and, thankfully, she didn't have to suffer through what was happening. I was forced to move too quickly, forced by my working full time and by my lack of a home big enough to to hold any of her lovely pieces and forced by my lack of a husband or sibling to help me and I was only one person. This was the only real home Leasa and I had ever known and it was still our home, too. Leasa helped me a lot but she was working full time, too, and we each had our own grief going on inside of us. I just kept on "keeping on" somehow chipping away at the job at hand that had to be done one day at a time and one hour at a time to get through it.

During all of this, I discovered yet another example of how some men treat women who have no husband. When I put Mother's home on the market the realtor talked me into letting him hire two painters he knew to paint the entire upstairs interior of the house. I came home one week-end to find quite a mess of "dribbles" the painters made around my bathroom's toilet. When I left I taped a note to the toilet that nicely stated, "Gentlemen, please wipe up any dribbles when finished." The very next day my realtor called me to tell me the two men quit the job right in the middle of it because my note made them so mad! I absolutely could not believe it! I told him to apologize to them and do whatever to get them back to finish the job. (Absurd knuckle-headed stubbornness always seems to find my doorstep and I wanted to stand on a high roof top and scream, "Give me a break!!!"

One night just before Mother died I was soundly sleeping on my stomach when suddenly it felt like I was being lifted up to the ceiling and it wasn't a dream. I was completely surrounded by a circle of what seemed like hooded monks in robes illuminated by a golden light. They did not speak but they transferred this thought to me, "Your mother does not have long to live." Then it felt as if I was lowered back down to the bed and I woke up sobbing. Mother died two weeks later. That was my third Pegasus Dream. Toni came immediately as she did when my brother died and when Kim died. I do not know what I would have done had it not been for Toni. She has been my friend since junior high school and was someone who knew me when...before all the defeats and battle scars. I'm sure silently she wonders what in Heaven's name is my problem! I know I certainly do! I began life with everything but a close relationship with the Lord and I think He was trying to get my attention and I'm so grateful that He did!

Three weeks from the day Mother died I was told that my teaching contract at a special school would not be renewed for the following year. I did not see that coming. It was my first teaching job and they had recruited me away from another job. They had also promised to back me up with any problems which they didn't do. They knew I was not a special education teacher and they hired me too late in the year for me to attend a required two weeks of classes to orient the teachers on all the special rules, regulations and procedures there. These students had plenty of discipline problems and I was the third art teacher in three years but I dealt with these problems effectively and things were working out very well I thought.

I believe I did an excellent job especially in view of the fact that I was given a zero budget and the teacher that replaced me was given a several thousand dollar budget I was told. Art supplies are extremely expensive and I had managed on almost nothing. I had called the local phone company and asked them to donate a big sack of plastic coated, colored wires which we used to make wire sculptures and the students loved it. I bought plaster and plastic face molds and let them pour the molds, dry them and paint them and they really liked having that project. I took a special light for them to use to draw each other's silhouette in profile to transfer onto black construction paper and some were wearing their cowboy hats which they also loved. The school delivered a kiln to my class room late in the year and I filled out a work order for them to install it but they never did.

After they told me I would not be re-hired for the next year I was then told they did not have to tell me why they were not renewing my contract because I had only been there for one year. Keep in mind I am a widowed single person who needed a job to survive! I genuinely cared about the students and about doing a good job. When the principal, who was also single, told me I was not being hired back for the next year I was trying to ask,"Why didn't you ever call me in and let me know you weren't pleased with my work?" but when I got out these words, "Why didn't you ever call me...", he interrupted me and said, "Oh, I was going to call you and ask you out but I never got around to it." I was struck into astonished silence! I couldn't even find my tongue to tell him what I was trying to say is, "why didn't you call me in to tell me you were unhappy with my work?", to correct his horrible assumption that I wanted him to call me on a personal basis! But I was in a state of shock and I couldn't get all the words out! How humiliating!!!

Why can't I ever think on my feet without loosing my tongue? I believe it was/is because I was taught from youth to always be respectful and never "speak up" since that was considered talking back. Looking back, I recall having to call in sick more than I wanted because my immune system was not yet building up against the students who carry all the latest viruses! I would go to bed feeling fine and wake up throwing up all day long. Maybe that's the reason but they could have told me if that were the case.

I felt extremely lost. All the lights in my life had burnt out except for Leasa, who was out of the nest but near by, thank Heavens! Between moments of this great and numbing grief clearer thoughts began coming to me. I could write volumes on the duality of my cowboy ex-husband and friends of Indian descent, from hindsight, which includes a few 'friends only' women friends, but I won't. Somehow I was a target and a vulnerable woman for "cowboys and Indians", the ones who have no hearts but who can be very charming and deceitful, I believe. I truly had no idea this kind of duplicity existed but actually it is just another trick of the devil's...but again, this was before I knew to consult the Lord about everything. I will never forget that the devil doesn't always look like the devil! We must always be aware of our daily fight with unseen principalities and the demons who attack us invisibly through addictions of all kinds, sinful desires, and every weakness known is made attractive and desirable through his lies. His goal is to kill and devour us and he roams the earth like a hungry lion.

I Peter 5:8, KJV, says, "Be sober be viligant; because your adversary the devil walks about like a roaring lion, seeking whom he may devour." And Ephesians 6:11 & 12, KJV, says, "Put on the whole armor of God that you may be able to stand against the wiles of the devil. For we do not wrestle against flesh and blood, but against principalities, and powers, against the rulers of the darkness of this age, against spiritual hosts of wickedness in the heavenly places."

I began reading my spiritual material again. I began fervently praying again. I believe this is KEY... that although I always believed myself to be a good Christian who tried to live by the Golden Rule I had been just barely touching the surface of living a Christ oriented life. I had been hurriedly going through the motions of living and doing the next chore in life that presented itself to me and crying myself to sleep a lot but I had not

154

been living prayerfully on a daily basis. I prayed before all this heartache but not constantly nor continuously and certainly never about important details and decisions of my life and I had failed to turn any of it over to the Lord! I didn't know that I could do that! This has to be the secret to living more completely for finding the strength to somehow go on. I began searching my soul deeply to know myself and to find my own part in all of this pain.

Thank the Lord that Mother left me an inheritance! I realize that ultimately it was Mother that literally saved my life and I am very grateful to her for this and for allowing me to have the childhood she never had however silent it may have been. I forgave my Mother because she could not give me the love and mothering she didn't have herself. I am thankful that I was finally able to convince her that I loved her but convincing her had not been an easy task. Still, I am very glad I didn't give up on her and, of course, all the credit goes to the Lord.

I decided to renew my Respiratory Therapy license and began working for a contract company for out of town nursing homes that October. Then that company left my area the following February.

Then Leasa became engaged to a young man and they planned to get married that summer. I had so hoped to have a husband by my side before she married to be there on this special day with me and for her. I'd buried most of my family all alone and now I had to marry my daughter alone. They decided to marry in a chapel in Amarillo and did so in July of 1996, in a very sweet and private family wedding. They even bought a darling home just two blocks from my house and I was so happy for her. May God always bless Leasa.

The following December brought more bad news...Leasa and her new husband were moving to San Antonio for a better job opportunity for him...500 miles away! I managed somehow to say good by to my precious Leasa but I died some more inside... this time almost totally. The light of my life was now gone very far away. I wasn't sure I had any reason to continue at all anymore.

On top of loosing Kim tragically, which made me a widow at 32, I'd lost my second mother, Darling Dickie in April, 1991; I lost my dear brother tragically in February, 1993; I'd lost my Mother in February 1995; I lost my job in February, 1995; and in 1996, my only child married and moved 500 miles away! I prayed with every breath...I prayed and read all the inspirational and spiritual material I could get my hands on...I prayed all the time...I kept on praying... praying daily...praying hourly...praying to put one foot in front of the other to literally get through the motions of daily living.

**** I even prayed to die, please forgive me,
Dear Lord! I really wanted to die and
I begged the Lord to please, please take me! ****

Literally my life became one long prayer. I ate, slept and prayed...ate, slept and prayed...slept, ate and prayed. It began to work. Very, very slowly I began to see a new life forming around me and it was as if I had been existing in and was emerging from a thick, thick fog. I still had not called out for Jesus' help out loud and let me stress that always makes an enormous difference!

A Respiratory Therapist friend of mine talked to me about applying for a therapy job at the hospital. I applied three times before they hired me in September, 1996. A merger had created several openings so I trained and oriented. I studied and learned. I followed seasoned therapists and learned to do arterial blood gas sticks (a new skill for me) and I began to feel like a new person. It had been twenty years since I had worked in a hospital and they now work twelve hour shifts instead of eight hour shifts. Even eight hour shifts had been physically very demanding twenty years ago constantly running all over the hospital but I kept at it until I caught the flu and a cycle of stomach flu and respiratory flu came and went back and forth for two months. My resistance to hospital viruses and infections would not build back up and I couldn't stay well. Fortunately as a temporary employee I could take some time off to get well which I did and then I returned to work shorter shifts. I didn't know I had Rheumatoid Arthritis yet but my knees had really hurt me badly ever since Leasa and I moved back to the Panhandle in 1987, and I lived on so much aspirin every day that my ears constantly rang. RA is an auto immune system disease and I had been catching hospital viruses very easily and could not get my immunities to hospital viruses built up like they did when I was younger. I also *almost* became ill listening to patients describe their symptoms to me due to some kind of sympathetic/empathetic overdrive sensitivity I have!

How many times can someone start completely

over in life? A friend of mine always says, "until you get it right." I believe that whatever a parent fails to teach a child life itself will teach them but it is the hardest way to learn and, undoubtedly, the most expensive, painful way by far. By not being married I had cost Leasa a father and myself a home and a complete family with a husband and caused her to lack knowing the best fellows to select as good, Christian family man for a future husband for herself. The harder and faster I worked the more quickly the years went by and the further away these goals moved from me. I never really learned to set goals and to focus on them and to work towards them. I just thought that things worked out like they were supposed to and that I've always been blessed...but I felt like Job in the Bible must have felt! I never knew to pray, or just talk to Jesus and ask Him for His will to be done in my life nor did I read and study the Bible *yet*. The Bible is a Living Bible because God Is the Word, and The Word became Flesh...so we embrace and get to know Him just by reading The Bible and He is our salvation therefore the Bible is our education and our contact with Him.

My life has been much like a giant roller coaster

ride with only one seat for one person...me. I had to make some sense of this giant puzzle called my life that was now heaped at my feet in a mess...this quest was the birth of "Cowboys and Indians and Pegasus Dreams". Pegasus is also from Revelations 6:2, which symbolizes Christ on a white horse Who actually has always been by my side from the beginning...it just took me awhile to *SEE* Him and to submit to and follow Him.

CHAPTER 8

LOST THEN FOUND

In the Fall of 1996, a close friend and former pathology partner of Kim's, V.K.'s, (may he rest in peace) daughter was seriously ill and in the hospital where I was working. I heard the overhead page for her family to return to their room which is how I knew they were there. (This was a God thing because they rarely paged for family by name..but they did that night.) I have known her since she was a child so I went to visit her after she got home and during this visit V.K. told me something very important that I never knew. I think he might never have told me except that he knew I still mourned Kim.

V.K. said that Kim was one of the pathologists in the E.R at Parkland Hospital when President Kennedy arrived, which I already knew that much. What he said next is what I never knew which is that they had done an initial exam and were about to begin a postmortem or autopsy when the secret service, the F. B. I., and the C.I.A. barged in and halted everything and they took the President's body to Bethesda Hospital for the official autopsy. He said they strongly warned all the attending doctors severely to never release ANY of their findings. As I understood it, the initial but incomplete postmortem exam itself was never to be disclosed as having even happened at all.

I then remembered a day when Kim and V.K. stopped by my apartment one afternoon in 1974. I remember the year because I was studying for my final exam before graduating from RT school. Kim was extremely disturbed about something and all he would tell us is that he'd found out something the night before that was so dangerous that his very life was in danger just for knowing about it! We tried to get him to tell us but he was white as a sheet and he never would say a thing more than that. Not one word more! Now I knew that it had to be related to that horrible day in Dallas when JFK was killed and V.K. confirmed this was true.

I also remembered that long ago Kim reluctantly told me he was one of a team of pathologists who did the autopsy on Lee Harvey Oswald. He said he was doing his pathology internship at Parkland Hospital in Dallas and he had just returned from lunch when the hospital was exploding with all the excitement of the assassination. He told me he saw the First Lady and Mrs. Connally and how chaotic the hospital was with secret service people, policemen and reporters. He said it was a mad house, of course, and that they used his office for the television crews to set up. Why in Heaven's name I never asked him more about Kennedy, I will never know. I always thought the President was dead on arrival and it just didn't occur to me to ask him about it and this was not a subject Kim wanted to discuss...at all...and that was the only time he ever spoke about it to me.

It took awhile for this revelation to sink in but it explained so much. I knew Kim didn't have a dual personality disorder. Gregarious and fun loving socially, yes, but he had been living with a horrible secret about which he had feared for his very life! I now think this was the reason he had no intention of ever remarrying fearing that through this knowledge he could bring danger upon his family. I also knew beyond a doubt that it was the reason he began drinking heavily which is what led to his death at only forty two. I was right about my gentle giant all along...that he was kind and dear just like I knew he was. He was a brilliant man living with a deadly secret while refusing to live "a life of quiet desperation." I wonder how many other lives have felt the repercussions of this one tragic murder? Who would have thought that this secret, which severely altered, if not ruined Kim's life, would emerge out of the blue nineteen years after his death and thirty four years after the assassination to touch his widow.

Fast forward to August 31, 2018, my friend, Cathy, invited me to hear a retired Amarillo physician speak at her Rotary Club's Friday luncheon as he was the last living physician that treated JFK that horrible day in Dallas. The physician gave his account about being the first doctor in the ER when JFK arrived. I won't go into details about what he said to avoid accidentally misquoting him. He did say that all the many physicians who attended to JFK were on a special list and he recalled Kim's name when I asked him about it. He said all of the doctors were held for a long time that day and were strongly warned not to ever say one word about what they'd seen regarding JFK, especially about the bullet wounds and their number and placement. I'd heard there is a law in Texas that they must do an autopsy in a case like this and he said this is correct. He also said that 118 people died untimely and unusual deaths within a short time after this and he confirmed that all the doctors were extremely alarmed and warned...exactly like I've always believed. I didn't ask him why he felt comfortable speaking about this now.

I am very glad I know the truth. It has, like they say, set me free. All these years I wondered if he had a death wish when I saw him push himself to extremes. How he could have kept such enormous and major secrets I will never know. Kim really was all the wonderful things I knew him to be. It just all finally came crashing down on him and in his desperate search for sweet forgetfulness he became a victim to the drink and to this deadly secret and his self-enforced, and otherwise enforced, silence. I believe I did not recognize the red flags of heavy drinking because I was reared around adults who drank and sometimes, they drank a lot. I realized he had an out of control problem with alcohol only after we were married and I naively believed I could help him with this.

After I recovered from the initial shock of Kim's death at first I responded by driving rather fast drinking a bit more at first but right away I thought of my precious little 7 year old daughter and I knew I had a really major reason to keep going. Then I realized life is like a thread of the finest silk which might blow away with the next gust of wind. So I began living gently thinking I would meet the same kind of like-minded people! Instead I was lambasted with this and that, the hurry, hurry, hurry of life which, I guess, helped me from thinking about my grief so much but it's not a good way to help anyone heal because it just delays the grief we each go through in our own ways.

I'd felt so much regret for never having the real home for Leasa and myself and for not finding the loving, Christian husband and father for her that I wanted so badly...and when I did find him, he was suddenly jerked from me tragically before I could even embrace him for even a moment in time! My biggest problem was that I always knew I was a Christian, and I was, but I was hardly skimming the surface of Christianity and I had no personal relationship with Christ! I was seeking everything but Christ and putting everything before Him, which I now know is idolatry, and failing to read His Holy Word. I was not yet a born again Christian and didn't yet know that nothing works without Christ...

absolutely nothing!!! And to always ask for "His Will, not mine" to be done is the only way to live successfully by surrendering completely to Him.

Another major blow came in June of 1998. I needed to get off my feet so I found a desk job at a commercial, non-medical business. It is very rare to find a desk job with my medical background in R.T. which is similar to an R.N. seeking a job outside a hospital and or a medical setting. Even working the short shifts running non-stop all over the hospital was damaging to my knees which hurt even when I was off my feet because I have Rheumatoid Arthritis. When the barometric pressure goes down just one point it causes flu like body aches. I was making a third of the pay I made at the hospital and worked triple the hours at this job but I got off my feet!

Problems began from the very first week when my immediate supervisor, who was single, began asking me out socially. He wasn't even asking, rather he was telling me, to go get a beer with him after work and to meet him at the swimming pool at his apartment the first week-end I worked there. I didn't go, of course, and he expected a full explanation for why I wasn't there! I know that dating or seeing one's boss socially is not ever the right thing to do. But rather than bluntly state this to him I always made up "polite" excuses. I was very strictly brought up never to talk back to people especially not to those in authority and I had not yet "found my tongue" to speak up for myself especially in disagreements or important confrontations. I believed he would take the hint and stop trying but that did not happen and he began getting very rude and abrupt with me after I'd refused him every time he told me to meet him over the first two months I worked there.

After my supervisor came up behind me at my desk and began rubbing my neck I finally got up the nerve later that day to tell him that I sensed something was wrong and asked if I was performing the job to his and my other boss's satisfaction. Assured by both that I was doing a good job I then asked my higher level boss (who was his boss, too) in private to please ask him to stop asking me out socially because it made me very uncomfortable. That boss answered, "WHY, he's a nice guy! You ought to go out with him!" The next day both bosses gave me a very hard time over a minor matter of faxing a letter. Even a boss over another area near the fax machine made a sympathetic comment to me something about the other bosses acting like "boys". I knew I could not please them on the job now no matter how hard I tried and I resigned the next morning by letters I delivered before anyone had arrived.

The personnel department called me in and asked me to explain my resignation and asked me not to resign. They placed me in another department into a temporary position. Long story made short, from there I was cold shouldered and ignored, told to watch for openings and to apply for a permanent position but when I found one and applied for it they did not even interview me. Instead I was demoted to a file clerk position which required a lot of bending and stooping and lifting and shoving heavy shelves.

The worst thing happened around Halloween when three of the highest level bosses carried a life sized, cut-out poster of President Clinton holding a real cigar around the area where the secretary's desks were and they paraded it around the floor then left it standing there for several days not long after that horrible story made news. Just the 'Good ol' Boys' having fun!

Fortunately, Leasa and her husband had moved back home and gave me the greatest gift possible...a precious Granddaughter! When my beautiful Granddaughter, Brittney, was born I was at the hospital for her birth by C-section. I watched through the surgery window while my fellow Respiratory Therapists worked on her a few minutes because she needed a little oxygen after her birth. Because I had worked at the hospital they let me scrub up and put on a gown and mask and stand by her crib in the Neonatal ICU. When she wrapped her tiny hand around my little finger and I stood there in awe staring at this wonderful miracle. I listened to her little heart with a stethoscope and just stared at her. I stayed by her side for awhile then I ordered pizzas for the Respiratory Therapy night shift to celebrate! The next day I held her on my lap on a pillow in Leasa's room for 4 hours until her great grandparents, Great Mother and J. Dear, arrived to see her and so, of course, I had to share her. I had found true love and my heart was certainly healing. Love really is the best Rx there is and we know that God is love!

When Leasa asked me if I would keep her full time while she worked I was elated! I gladly resigned that job knowing successful employment there was not possible. I was happier being a full time grandmother than with anything else I've ever done and I got to stay at home and keep Brittney from the time she was six weeks old until after she started middle school. After she started school Leasa would drop her off in the mornings and

I got her ready and took her to school and picked her up afterward. I also got to keep her while her mother traveled two weeks a year on her job and full time in the summers, which I absolutely loved having her as much time as possible and this became the favorite part of my life.

This is so special but is hard to write about but I must because it led to a wonderful miracle! I kept Brittney until a regrettable misunderstanding happened between Leasa and me in mid July of 2009, and my heart began breaking again. I offended Leasa when I told her they should take a gun on their camping trip in the Pecos wilderness because I knew bears would smell their cooking and I'd recently seen a bear at a friend's cabin in New Mexico! I think it frightened and upset her and her reaction to me and my reaction to her led to an unfortunate arguement and my being abruptly "let go" as her nanny. The light of my life had, again, been yanked from me and there wasn't anything I could do about it...and I tried everything I could think of to reconcile...all to no avail. I fell asleep sobbing, woke up sobbing and I sobbed several times a day. I cried so much I gave myself a sinus infection but I'd never had sinus problems before so I didn't know what it was.

Heartbreak can cause all kinds of health problems, I would not include this sad story but it led me to having the most amazing supernatural dream...my fourth 'Pegasus Dream'.

****The following paragraphs ought
to be printed in pure gold!****

Then I was blessed to have this most realistic and miraculous experience in a dream where I was going down a long dark tunnel and traveled way, way back in time until I was looking, though a bit distantly, at the *actual Crucifixion of Christ* through a dark sky and dark clouds. I was slightly behind the three crosses on the hill and to His left. And I swear this is true, as God is my Witness! I was actually being permitted to *see His Sacred Sacrifice!* Thank you, Precious Lord!!!

I believe I'd cried so many purifying tears for so long that I was allowed to witness the actual crucifixion in a dream. Please read those words again and think about what I just said. I had suffered so much pain that I was supernaturally taken back in time to witness the actual crucifixion....*I repeat... I had suffered so much pain & cried so many purifying tears that I was supernaturally taken back in time to witness the actual Crucifixion!* The Lord still performs miracles even today and that was an awesome miracle!

When I woke up and thought about it I realized that the message from Him is that no matter what kind of pain nor how many tears I (or any of us) might suffer through in life nothing, and I mean absolutely nothing, compares to the pain that Christ suffered for each one of us sinners so that we may someday see Him in Heaven and avoid the burning pit of Hell for all eternity! Thank you, Lord, for allowing me to distantly witness the one Event, a Holy Event, in all of history that saves all our souls if we believe. But it is our choice and He doesn't force us to accept Him as our Savior. This is the grandest Gift all and I am not worthy to receive it nor is anyone else. It is entirely through His Amazing Grace, which I claim over all my entire life and over my family and loved ones that we are allowed to pray and to worship Him.

Yet another nightmare came in 2005, when my stockbroker was indicted for doing Ponzi schemes. He was from my hometown and I'd known him and his family all my life. His client list was very impressive which is why I selected him in in spite of his reputation. He kept most of his wealthy clients safe and just did the Ponzi scheme on people like his immediate family, my daughter and myself and a million dollars from a local business. So we had to get an attorney and fight yet another legal battle! What a scary ordeal that lasted fifteen months! It turned out that the Lord had, again, gone before us and kept us safe totally through a legal quirk, praise the Lord, and my good friend, Tricia, who introduced me to Bible Study Fellowship International just before this all began which is what saved my sanity during those agonizing months. My entire adult life has been a legal nightmare and I prayed this was the last of legal problems. I purposely did not name specific parties here because I'm not seeking revenge with this book... that is the Lord's job.

I want to give a special thank you to my friend, Mike Harrington, our high school class Valedictorian, Yale graduate, studied at Cambridge then graduated Harvard Law School, and attorney who recently retired from a prestigious law firm in Houston. He was extremely helpful to hear my situation and offer his and a partner of his best legal advice pro bono for me. Thank you, Mike, for being such a giving, loyal friend. God bless you and your family. Many thanks as you truly went far beyond the call of friendship for me.

I've had to live a life of a single woman in a man's world where I've been treated as if I were invisible and didn't count at all. I always prayed daily but I didn't know I needed to have been on my knees and seeking Christ through His Living Word. I didn't know that until Bible Study Fellowship, Inc. What a shame and loss of precious time! But what a *treasure*!!! I found God, the Father, the Great I AM. Praise His Holy Name for leading me here however painful it may have been, finding Him was worth every bit of the suffering! I am grateful for this opportunity to speak up against things like this in effort to help change the world for our children and our children's children.

I finally found my pony, Pegasus, after going through everything. Pegasus represents the white horse symbolizing Christ's conquering fight in Revelations 6:2, KJV, and He carried me through my past while I wrote about my shattered life and as I picked up these shining bits of love and humor here and there and as He brought me to my knees to receive my Savior Jesus Christ. And now I ask God's favor, forgiveness and blessings for all those who have gone before me and who have traveled, part way, by my side, and always for my precious family and friends. And one day I believe

He will carry us all to a better place where all are honest people who are genuinely happy for one another and who genuinely love and care for one another without hidden agendas...where people strive to do the right thing for the right reasons to and for everyone their lives touch...and, most importantly, who know how to show love. Jesus Himself commanded us to "do unto others as we would have others do unto us. And to love our neighbors as ourselves." When we seek Him through reading His Word we actually invite Him into our hearts and souls, where He dwells through the Holy Spirit. What an awesome blessing!

My prayer for my loved ones and me is for God's grace and abundant mercies and blessings to be upon us and for His divine guidance, protection and wisdom to grace our lives always. I end with these scriptures, "Learn to do good, seek justice, rescue the oppressed, defend the orphan, and plead for the widow." Isaiah 1:17, KJV, and "Whatever you do, do everything for the glory of God." I Corinthians 10:31, KJV. And for all my numerous losses due to these mean hearted people causing me to start my life over & over again, I refer to Philippians 3:8, NKJV, "Yet indeed I also count all things loss for the excellence of the knowledge of Christ Jesus my Lord, for whom I have suffered the loss of all things, and count them as rubbish, that I may gain Christ."

--------------------After Thoughts--------------------

Just before Kim died I made a tiny clay sculpture of him in his week end "uniform"...his blue jeans and denim shirt with his leather vest and he's holding a giant UT orange glass in this hand. Since then I've made many of these caricatures and have given them as gifts to special people but Kim's was the first one I made. My painting and my sculpture have served to help keep my sanity in this insane world just like it did for dear Cloe, who gave me these gifts.

After all these years I have finally found true joy and true love in Jesus. I actually find myself humming and singing out loud around the house which I've never done before until now. If I am sad I start praising Him and my day is renewed. I've found the fruit of the Holy Spirit mentioned in Galatians 5:22-23, KJV, "The fruit of the Spirit is love, joy, peace, long suffering, gentleness, goodness, faith, meekness, temperance, against such there is no law." May we all find this.

by Catherine Ann

Mike's Great Frog Hunt

Tubby Time for Bob Cobb

My fifth 'Pegasus Dream' came when our dear friend and family physician, Dr. Woody, passed away on a Christmas morning. I dreamed of him as he left the earth and soon after his wife called with the sad news. He taught me to drive a car in his brand new, red Pontiac Firebird when I was 14 and I loved him and his family like my own.

Psalms: 30-5; KJV says, "Weeping may endure for a night but joy cometh in the morning." Kim's mother gave me a button jar and she cross stitched this scripture onto the covered lid.

Job 5:17 & 18, KJV says, "Behold, happy is the man whom God correcteth; there despise not thou the chastening of the Almighty. For He maketh sore, and bindeth up; He woundeth and His hands make whole."

Revelation 3:12, KJV says, "Him that overcometh I will make a pillar in the temple of my God."

One Last Story

One weekend in June after my many losses I offered to watch my friend, Cathy's, antiques store on Sixth Street for her. It was completely quiet and I was all alone in the shop when I heard the front door open. I walked around to the other side of the store and was amazed to see wet footprints on the floor but it wasn't raining or wet outside that day nor was there any standing water outside, nor had it rained recently so I searched the entire store and found no one and returned to the wet footprints where I discovered a yellow slip of paper the size of a business card on the floor by the footprints. On the front was the symbol of the fish. And inside the symbol was written, "Follow me and I will make you become fishers of men." Mark 1:17, NKJV, and I still have it, of course. Perhaps He has made me a "fisher of men" through my writing. I hope so.

Daddy was a fisherman who often said, "Be of good cheer!", to everyone he met. This is from John 16:33, NKJV, "Be of good cheer for I have overcome the world." And to that I say, "Ditto, Daddy! Ditto!" He also often said for some unknown reason, "That's all she wrote!" And to that I say, "for now, anyway."

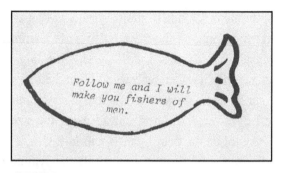

I want to end with a blessing for all in the form of this wonderful song, "The Love of God", which I hope you will hear. You can hear this wonderful song and read about the third stanza being found scratched on the wall of a German Asylum in 1917, by an unknown prisoner who had been put to death. The rest of the song is by F.M. Lehman and his daughter, Mrs. W.W. Mays. https://www.youtube.com/watch?v=k6B_jYtjvME.